LOOKING FOR SOM
DIFFERENT IN MIC

A SAMPLING OF THE MANY "SOMETHING DIFFERENT" PLACES IN OUR BOOK!

How about a unique island adventure?

Try our Bois Blanc Island home where the setting is natural, the populations sparse, the beaches open and the wildlife abundant (Region 2)!

Ride off into the sunset on a Michigan dude ranch!

You'll find plenty to keep you busy at the Double JJ Resort in Rothbury (Region 6) with horses and trails for the inexperienced to pro, *plus* — archery and rifle ranges, a champion ship golf course, nightly entertainment — and 24 hour non-stop activities ! Or, for more family-styled fun, try the Double "R" Ranch, in Smyrna (Region 6) ...Yee-haw!

This is for the birds ... watchers, that is !

Nettie Bay Lodge, in Hawks (Region 2), features birding seminars, workshops and nature walks on weekends throughout the summer!

Stay in an Earl Young style boulder home in beautiful Charlevoix!

The history behind the Earl Young Boulder cottages is well known throughout the area. Now you can stay at a comfortable getaway built in Mr. Young's own unique style (Region 5).

A little sampling of the Michigan grape!

Stay at Château Chantel B&B — northern Michigan's only operating vineyard, winery and bed and breakfast! Sip wine and enjoy the scenic views from this hilltop estate on Old Mission Peninsula in the Traverse City area (Region 5).

Do you want to catch that fish — you know, the one that got away?

Take one of the guided fishing boat charters available to guests at the Lac La Belle Resort on Thousand Island Lake in Watersmeet (Region 4).

A bit of elegance in the wilderness ... snowmobile out the door ...

Teal Wing and Mallard Cove are your private vacation homes on Lake Gogebic (Region 4) which provide *all* the amenities and ... a snowmobile trail just outside your door ... great biking, hiking, fishing and swimming, too!

1995-96

Michigan Vacation Guide

Cottages, Chalets, Condos, B&B's

THIRD EDITION

Editor: Kathleen R. Tedsen

Associate Editor: Clara M. Rydel

Feature Writer/Photographer: Beverlee J. Rydel

Business Manager: Christian E. Tedsen

Michigan

Statehood: 1837   25th State of the Union

Let me take you to the land once called "Michigania" across flat planes to ever increasing slopes, hills and mountains; through virginal forests and crystal lakes, dotted by cottages resting on sugar white sand. Where falls are painted by an artist's brush and winters are blanketed in white. Here are the forests and wildlife, quaint cities and great cities, museums and shipwrecks, and so much more!

I am your dream maker ...
the great outdoors ...
the vacation land for all seasons!

HOW TO USE THIS BOOK

Welcome to our third edition of *The Michigan Vacation Guide to Cottages, Chalets, Condos, B&B's*! This simple to use publication, arranged by region and alphabetically by city, is designed to assist you with one of your first vacation priorities — WHERE TO STAY — and offers some interesting alternatives to the usual hotels/motels. We hope our Guide helps you find your perfect vacation lodging as quickly and effortlessly as possible.

WHAT'S NEW FOR 1995-96?

Editor's Note   Our staff has not had the opportunity to visit every listing in this book. Many of the descriptions have been supplied by owners or chambers of commerce. When we have visited a lodging, we have made comments at the bottom of the listing by using *Editor's Note*.

Editor's Choice indicates places our staff have visited which, in our opinions, exceeds the basic requirements of comfort, cleanliness, location and value.

MORE REVIEWS! We've significantly increased our Review Section to include more vacation lodgings, photographs and detail. All comments are solely the opinion of our staff and do not necessarily reflect the opinions of others.

ALL DAILY OR WEEKLY RENTAL PRICES ARE SUBJECT TO CHANGE.

Whenever possible, prices have been included. One thing you should remember, prices frequently change or fluctuate with the seasons. We recommend you call to verify rates when making your reservations. If the owner requires an advance deposit, verify refund policies (if any). As a renter, be sure you understand the terms of the rental agreement.

Thanks...

To the many property owners who have given their support .... and our many readers for their helpful comments and suggestions! Hope we continue to hear from you! And another BIG THANKS to the Michigan Travel Bureau for their continued support!

REGIONAL DIVISIONS

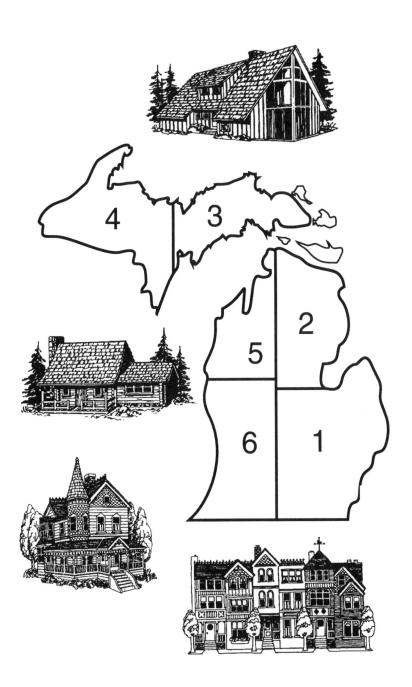

TABLE OF CONTENTS

REGION 3 (continued...)

REGION 4

REGION 5

REGION 6

Reviews

MICHIGAN COTTAGES • CHALETS • CONDOS • B&B'S

MICHIGAN LODGING REVIEWS

During the past summers and falls, our travels took us to many wonderful locations and interesting lodgings throughout Michigan.

The following reviews are a selection of those accommodations we visited. Please note, the comments made, unless otherwise noted, are based on visual inspections only. Also, realizing that everyone's vacation needs are different, we wish to emphasize that all reviews are based solely on our writers' personal opinions and may not reflect the opinions of others!

Best wishes for a great Michigan vacation!

STILLMEADOWS BED & BREAKFAST
CAROL LATSCH, ONAWAY (REGION 2)
(517) 733-2882

Carol Latsch, born and raised in the Onaway area, has turned this attractive, large, country home into a bed and breakfast to supplement her teaching income.

The amiable hostess loves exchanging stories with her guests, especially hunters, since her father was an avid outdoorsman. The house and rooms reflect her interest in nature and animals. The soft earth tone furniture in the sitting area is highlighted by a large wall tapestry of a deer. The large comfortable sitting/dining area is airy with plenty of large windows

Quite country setting

for viewing the well landscaped yard, woods and wildlife around her house. The bedrooms, all located upstairs, are large and comfortable with patchwork quilts in browns, rusts and forest greens. We spent the night in a bright, cheery room with two comfortable twin beds and large window overlooking the front yard. It

Comfortable guest rooms

also had table and chairs with a private bath, distinctive with large octagon stained glass window.

In the morning we woke to the crowing of Carol's rooster and the aroma of bacon, homemade muffins and brewing coffee. Breakfast was hearty and wonderful, a real hunter's meal. It started with fresh strawberries, blueberries, kiwi, apples, peaches, and a variety of other seasonal fruit. Our second course consisted of bacon or sausage, eggs (from her own chickens), muffins or toast and pastries. Some mornings you may find pancakes or waffles. Of course she has juices and cereals if you prefer. Eating at our window table, we enjoyed watching her dogs and chickens in the backyard. We hoped to see some deer, elk, or fox, but no luck that morning. Over breakfast Carol filled us in on the numerous hunting and fishing spots as well as local shopping and attractions in Onaway and the surrounding area. Not far from Mackinaw, there is plenty do in the area. For about $40-$45 a night, this B&B is worth a visit. No pets or smoking permitted.

3

GRAM MCGEORGE, PRIVATE HOME
BOIS BLANC ISLAND (REGION 2)
(616) 846-4391

W e have discovered a great retreat on an island which happens to be one of Michigan's best kept secrets — Bois Blanc! Only reached by ferry from Cheboygan, it is quiet and surrounded in wilderness — a direct contrast from the hustle and bustle found on its immediate neighbor, Mackinac Island. With the help of Jeremy McGeorge, son of the property's owners,

McGeorge's secluded home

and long time island resident, Janie Galbraith, we learned quite a bit about Bois Blanc.

The island's name was originally chosen by its early French settlers and translates into *White Woods* (so named because of its abundance of white birch). Today there are approximately 40 to 50 year around residents with populations growing to 200 during summer months. It has a one-room schoolhouse (K-8), still in use, two small grocery stores, the Boat House Restaurant and Bois Blanc Tavern. All are great spots to meet the friendly locals.

The main road, unpaved, is easily traversed. The many secondary roads require four wheel drive vehicles and, with four lakes on the island, it's a great place for fishing or just exploring! There's also plenty of tame wild life here and, as Janie said, "They're like our pets". Its historic light-

View of natural, open beach area

house, built in 1829, was known as the hide-a-way for notorious John Dillinger. In the winter, island residents spike a trail across the frozen waters

McGeorge (continued...)

of the Huron (the ice must be at least 16 inches thick) to allow snowmobiles to reach the main land. This is their only access to Cheybogan during the winter. For safety, to make sure the residents use the proper trail, it is lined with pine trees.

The McGeorge's island retreat is a terrific place to base your Bois Blanc adventure! This two story home was built around 1985. The McGeorge's have owned it since 1993. The well maintained exterior is nestled in a very natural, untouched setting and is surrounded by large trees and wild grass. The driveway is narrow and unpaved — keep your eyes open or you'll miss it because of the many trees lining the street! The property is approximately 1/2 acre with nearly 400 feet

Clean and comfortable interior

of beach front. The beach is also natural with wild grass growing out of the pure white sand and features good swimming in the summer.

The first floor of the home is bright, airy, cheerful and offers a fully equipped kitchen (including microwave and dishwasher), laundry area with washer/dryer, plus small bedroom and full bath. For those hot afternoons, there is a shaded, screened, furnished sunporch. Its living/dining area features white walls, white and pink striped furniture, fireplace, new gray carpeting and an expansive wall of windows overlooking Lake Huron.

The second floor consists of two bedrooms. Renovations were going on in those rooms during our visit and held much promise (they should be completed by 1995)! Both bedrooms are large with two queen and three double beds. We found the cottage immaculate, airy and very comfortably decorated.

The McGeorge's house is rented year around, with weekly rates ranging from $400 to $600. Ferry service to the island is approximately $40, round trip.

THE PINEWOOD LODGE B&B
JERRY & JENNY KRIEG
AUTRAIN (REGION 3)

(906) 892-8300

Jerry and Jenny Krieg were still in the process of building this very new log-styled lodge when we stopped to visit. It is surrounded by tall, stately Norway pine and rests on the sandy beach of Lake Superior.

Newly built Pinewood Lodge B&B

Enthusiastic about their progress, Jerry still was completing a few finishing touches to the lodge which will includes a gift shop for his wife's handmade crafts. Much of Jenny's finely crafted, creative wall and table decorations are made from driftwood found along the beaches of Lake Superior. Her work can not only be found in the lodge's gift shop but also in the guest rooms. The eight knotty pine rooms have a very comfortable, rustic styling with hand carved bed posts, country and hand-hewn furniture, and patchwork quilts. Five rooms have private baths while three share a bath. The *Honeymoon Room* comes with a champagne breakfast served in bed. Day or night, when it's time to relax, you'll be sure to enjoy the sauna, hot tub, spacious great room with fireplace and ... something a little different ... player piano. The media room is the place for some TV and music.

Comfortable, rustic-styled rooms

Our personal favorite feature of the lodge is the enormous deck surrounding the back of the home. It's just the place to ease back and look out across the 350 feet of pure white sandy beach to the lake. Weather permitting, this is where breakfast is often served — which make's Jenny's freshly prepared, hearty full breakfasts an even greater treat! Pinewood is a terrific get away. It is located between Marquette and Munising. Daily rates range from $75 to $110.

PALOSAARI'S ROLLING ACRES B&B
CLIFF & EVEY PALOSAARI
CHASSELL (REGION 4)
(906) 523-4947

A little different than most, this B&B is an operating dairy farm owned by the charming Evelyn and Clifford Palosaari who love to show you around the farm. Clifford will gladly give you a tour of the barn and let you watch or help milk the cows and Evelyn loves to walk you through her fruit and vegetable gardens offering you a sampling of whatever is in season. We can guarantee you her strawberries are great.

Palosaari's is also an operating farm

Just as charming as the couple are the rooms, light and airy with a modern country decor and shared baths. Unlike many B&B's they do permit well mannered children, who would probably enjoy seeing the farm in operation. There is a sauna available and of course they serve a full country breakfast.

Not far from Keweenaw, there is plenty of nearby shopping, swimming, hiking and snowmobile trails. A great little B&B with a slightly different twist. Call for rates.

GRASSO'S WEST SHORE RESORT
PAT & DEBBIE GRASSO
LAKE GOGEBIC (REGION 4)
(906) 842-3336

L ocated on the west shore of Upper Peninsula's largest lake, Lake Gogebic, Grasso's Resort is a great find. Pat and Debbie Grasso, the down to earth, hard working couple, are full of enthusiasm and ideas for their resort which they've recently acquired. When we visited, they had completed interior and exterior renovation of the cottages, and had done a very nice job!

GRASSO'S (continued...)

Grasso's cozy interior

Each unit's exterior was freshly painted with grill and lawn chairs in front. The four knotty pine cottages we saw were in very good condition. Each with comfortable, newer sofa and chairs. The kitchens were appealing with knotty pine cabinets, all cooking utensils, new refrigerators and stoves, plus new sets of matching dishes, cups, glasses and silverware. There was a table and chairs for dining. The bathrooms offered tubs and showers (linens and towels provided). There were TVs in each unit but no cable. The four cabins we saw had two small, but functional, bedrooms with double beds and good mattresses.

Set near to each other, the cottages rest on a clear section of land running perpendicular to the water and are surrounded by approximately five acres of treed land. A small gazebo is located in the center court along with volley ball and picnic tables. There is 300 feet of beach front with lawn furniture, boat launch and hoist. It is not a sandy beach. There is also a fish cleaning station and freezer. Boats and motors are available for rent.

Great fishing and scenic location

Lake Gogebic is a large, expansive sheet of deep blue surrounded by the natural beauty of the Upper Peninsula. One of the most beautiful lakes in the state, it is known for it's walleye, perch, northern pike and small mouth bass. There is plenty to see and do here in the summer and, naturally, this is a winter sport paradise for snowmobiling, ice fishing and cross country skiing. Pat and Debbie will gladly fill you in on all points of interest on the lake and surrounding area.

Weekly rates are very affordable, beginning at around $260 per week, based on two people. Winter rates are approximately $275. Daily rates are available. There is a $5 charge for each additional person.

SUNNYSIDE CABINS
LAKE GOGEBIC (REGION 4)

(906) 842-3371

Without a doubt, these were some of the finest cabins we saw in Region 4 — inside and out! In fact, the word "cabin" doesn't do them justice.

All fully renovated in the past one to three years, these lodgings offer a comfort and luxury not often found in traditional cabin settings! Located on over 300 ft. of beachfront on Lake Gogebic, each unit is comfortably spaced between trees with most facing the water. The grounds are natural, but well

maintained with picnic tables, grassy area for games, new private dock, boat launch and a swimming raft. New fishing boats and motors are available to rent.

The caretaker, Sue Grooms, does an excellent job of maintaining the eight units. The knotty pine interiors of the cabins we saw were new and absolutely spotless. The living/dining areas had new carpeting with very comfortable and well coordinated

New, well decorated interiors

sofa, chairs, tables and lamps. Each had satellite TV and a doorwall leading to the deck which faces the water. The dining tables were large pine picnic-styled with padded benches. Kitchens were bright with sparkling cabinets and linoleum floors and are fully equipped with refrigerator, stove, microwave, toasters, utensils and dishes. Bathrooms were appealing with tub and shower. Bedrooms had warm brown carpeting with full size beds that were firm and comfortable. Bed linens are provided.

Fully equipped kitchens

Try Sunnyside for a fun, comfortable getaway! Prices change with the season so it's best to call for rates. Pets are not allowed.

9

TEAL WING & MALLARD COVE
TOM & ARLENE SCHNELLER
LAKE GOGEBIC (REGION 4)

OFFICE: (906) 932-1411 HOME: (906) 932-2577

Without a doubt, this was our favorite spot in the Upper Peninsula because of it's interior comfort and scenic location — all at an extremely good price!

View between *Mallard Cove* & *Teal Wing*

Both *Teal Wing* and *Mallard Cove* are very new and were designed and built by Tom Schneller and his construction company. We stayed at *Teal Wing* (named for the teal colors throughout) and found it to have all the comforts of home and more. All three floors of the house are light, airy and perfectly decorated for eye-appealing comfort.

The first floor (lower level) of *Teal Wing* contained bunk beds for children and a recreation area with games, books, magazines, music, table, chairs and small sofa. Large windows look directly over the lake. The sleeping area is carpeted and the recreation area tiled. This is the perfect place for children or adults to play.

The second floor is the main living area. The kitchen has everything you need including phone, refrigerator with ice maker, microwave, etc. The teal counter tops are attractively accented with light oak cabinets and cream floors. It should be noted that light oak accents are used consistently throughout the house maintaining it contemporary, bright and airy feel. The living area contains TV, VCR, videos and small stereo unit and features teal carpeting, large oak dinner table and matching chairs. In the center of the room are two very comfortable, overstuffed sofas. Its free standing

Open interiors of *Teal Wing*

Teal Wing/Mallard Cove (continued...)

fireplace/franklin stove adds warmth to its contemporary appeal. The entire room is surrounded by an expanse of windows overlooking the scenic woods and lake. To the left of the living area is a large bedroom with double bed, light print spread, ceiling fan, tables and large closet. The mattress, as in all the bedrooms, is medium firm and very comfortable. The room's light and airy feel is enhanced by both the decor and long, spacious doorwall with deck facing the water. The comfortably sized bathroom (tub and shower) is highlighted in white, cream with teal accents.

Comfortable bedroom

The second floor contains two bedrooms and bath. The large bedroom on this level is almost identical to the one on the first floor, including doorwall and deck. It also has a private sink and vanity area. The smaller bedroom has two twin beds and full bathroom with tub and shower. New carpeting covers the first and second floor. This home comfortably sleeps eight.

The well maintained exterior rests in a natural setting surrounded by trees. It has a private dock with boat lift approximately fifty feet from the house (boats can be rented). There's plenty of wood for the fireplace near the back porch

Mallard Cove setting

and three fat and frisky raccoons for entertainment.

Mallard Cove is right next door, but not easily visible because of the trees. We were not able to visit *Mallard Cove,* but understand it is very similar in interior layout, features and comfort to *Teal Wing* and can also accommodate eight people. New carpeting, paint and decor updates were made in 1994. Both homes are available year around, by the week or weekends. They are located on snowmobile route #5 and not far from skiing. Weekly rates are around $800 to $900 dollars.

11

LAURIUM MANOR INN
JULIE & DAVE SPRANGER
LAURIUM (REGION 4)

(906) 337-2549

Laurium Manor Inn was originally built in 1908 at a cost of $50,000 with 40 rooms and over 13,000 square feet. Your hosts, Julie and Dave Spranger have owned this historic inn since 1989.

Impressive Laurium Manor Inn

Walking through its many rooms takes you back to the early 1900's when wealth and luxury were common in Copper Country. The Sprangers have effectively maintained its original appearance while adding updates for their guests' comfort and safety.

The king or queen size beds are framed with brass, mahogany or similar dark wood bed posts.

Every room is inviting and comfortable, decorated with antiques and memorabilia of the period. Most have private baths, two share a bath.

The dining room and sitting rooms are striking with their dark, rich woods, period furniture and light fixtures, marble fireplaces and leaded and stained glass windows. Some noteworthy features are the silver leaf covered ceilings of the music parlor, embossed and gilded elephant hide wall cov-

Elegant and inviting rooms

erings and the grand triple staircase of hand carved oak, just to name a few.

A light breakfast buffet of muffins, pastries, homemade bread, cereal, fresh fruit, coffee, tea, milk and juice is included. During the summer prices range from $50 to $100 per night. Winter rates are slightly lower. Guided tours of the Manor are available daily. It's definitely worth the visit.

KEWEENAW MOUNTAIN LODGE
Copper Harbor (Region 4)
(906) 289-4403

The Keweenaw Mountain Lodge, located at the tip of Copper Harbor, is about as far north in Michigan as you can go. The lodge, a focal point of the area, began in the late 1930's when the copper mines died out. At that time the county had an unemployment rate of over 70% and began developing the lodge as a means of employment for its people. Today it is still owned and operated by Keweenaw County, but has grown from its original pine log cabins and lodge to an expansive resort.

The approach to the resort is natural and beautiful. Moving along Highway 26 you'll pass several small but breathtaking

Great dining at the lodge

waterfalls, travel through densely wooded areas then, in this wilderness, you'll spot a stone fence, a groomed lawn and you're there!

The main lodge is the center of the resort and rests at the top of a hill. The restaurant here is definitely worth a visit! Dramatically accented with a 40 ft. high stone fireplace, the high gloss knotty pine interior and fine china with linen accents create a unique contrast. The panoramic view from the dining area is equally charming overlooking

Comfortable cabins

well groomed gardens and their world class 18 hole golf course. While there, we enjoyed several meals skillfully prepared by Chef, Mike Koski. Among his many specialities are freshly prepared fish and prime rib. For those with hearty appetites, the prime rib, served in a light au jus, will definitely be a favorite!

Nestled in the treed hillside are the log cabins and motel units, many built in the 1930's. All are clean, in good condition with private baths and one to three bedrooms with two double beds. Several have fireplaces. The living rooms are large, with hard wood floors and serviceable though older chairs and sofas. There are no kitchens. At night, from your cabin, you might see a bear or two strolling among the trees. The cabins start at about $55 daily. The Lodge should be a "must visit" when in the Keweenaw Peninsula!

LAMBERT'S CHALET, COTTAGES AND VACATION HOMES, RICHARD LAMBERT
ONTONAGON (REGION 4)
(906) 884-4230

Resting amongst the trees and wilderness along the shores of Lake Superior you'll find the lodgings of Richard Lambert. From rustic one room cabins to open chalets and log styled homes accommodating up to two families, each well maintained lodging offers something different!

One of Lambert's newer cabins

The four units we saw were in very good condition, inside and out. The oldest but largest unit, *Cedar Lodge*, can easily hold two families. Some of its furniture was older, yet still comfortable. The fully equipped kitchen included microwave and dishwasher and for your relaxation there was a Jacuzzi and large deck.

Pine Lodge, a newer two story pine cabin with upstairs loft bedroom and two downstairs bedrooms, was our favorite! The craftsmanship inside is exquisite with special hand carved doors and railings. It had an inviting stone fireplace in the large comfortable living room and a doorwall and deck overlooking Lake Superior. Another favorite was the smaller one bedroom unit, *Gitche Gumee.* Light and cheerful with a beautiful, large stone fireplace in the living room, it would be the perfect spot for a couple's retreat with spacious bedroom, queen size bed, sofa bed and new kitchen.

Interior decor varies with units

Several miles away stands the three story, A-frame chalet. Its open, glass front offers a picturesque view of Lake Superior across the street. This chalet was elegantly furnished and comfortable. The 3-story fireplace adds a dramatic accent. This is a beautiful home well worth the $200 plus a night. There are 15 units ranging in price from $50 to $215 per night. All lodgings includes phone, TV and full baths.

14

MICHIGAMME LAKE LODGE B&B
FRANK & LINDA STABILE
CHAMPION (REGION 4)

(800) 358-0058

Off the main highway down a heavily wooded yet well manicured drive is the historic Michigamme Lake Lodge overlooking the Upper Peninsula's second largest lake, Michigamme. It was built in 1934 and is currently owned by Frank and Linda Stabile.

This two story, authentic pine lodge is perfectly landscaped and nearly hidden by tall white birch. The deep blue waters of the lake are surrounded by the natural beauty of the region. With 1700 feet of lake frontage, the lodge's sandy beach and shallow waters make for great swimming. If you prefer, take one of their canoes out for some excellent fishing.

The pine interior of the lodge is graced with the rugged elegance of the tall stone fireplace and original Indian carpets covering the walls and railing of the second floor. The stone in the fireplace and nearly all the wood in the lodge are from the immediate area. Throughout you

Inviting interior of lodge

will find many antiques reminiscent of mining and logging days of the past. The 40 ft. sunporch faces south over the water and is furnished with adirondack chairs and tables. The rooms, many overlooking the lake, have authentic log furniture, are well decorated and comfortable. Some have

Comfortable, rustic-styled guest rooms

private baths. To top it off, in the morning you'll be greeted to the warm and inviting aroma of freshly prepared hot cinnamon waffles and homemade nut bread — who can resist? Rooms range from $60 to $125.

MICHIGAN COTTAGES • CHALETS • CONDOS • B&B'S

LAC LA BELLE RESORT
SKIP & CARYL BUCHANAN
WATERSMEET (REGION 4)
(906) 358-4396

Because of its natural beauty and abundance of wildlife, Thousand Island Lake is one of our favorite spots in the Upper Peninsula. As a result, Lac La Belle is in an excellent location! These well maintained, year round cottages are nestled on Thousand Island Lake (part of the Cisco Chain of Lakes) with each having a good view of the water. Skip and Caryl Buchanan have operated the resort for 10 years and love their work.

All cottages are heated and have two bedrooms. The units we viewed were clean, comfortable and in good repair. Their kitchens were fully equipped with cozy knotty pine cabinets, functional refrigerators and stoves. Much of

Great fishing & boating

Simple but comfortable interiors

the woodworking was done by Skip. The furnishings, consisting of couch and one or two stuffed chairs, were comfortable (linens and blankets provided, except for towels). Exterior maintenance on the cabins was acceptable. Skip and Caryl plan on remodeling several units by 1995.

Additional features at the resort include a fire pit, fish cleaning station, and freezer. Boats are available for guests. Of course, fishing on the Chain is excellent — from Walleye and Musky to Perch and Trout. Lac La Belle also offers guide service. These comfortable and affordable cabins rent for about $400 per week.

HAMLET VILLAGE CONDOMINIUMS & RESORT HOMES
HARBOR SPRINGS (REGION 5)
(616) 526-2641

S ophisticated, contemporary country comfort—this is Hamlet Village Resort. Set in various locations in the rolling hills of Harbor Springs, these vacation condos and homes are a excellent vacation hideaway!

Private and well placed condo units w/Nubs Nob access

Features include heated pool, whirlpool, sauna and tennis courts plus, an added bonus at the condominiums, *"Ski-in, Ski-out"* access to Nubs Nob! This is a real benefit considering there are currently no lodgings available on Nubs Nob's premises! Excellent skiing is also available at Boyne Highlands only 1/2 mile away.

The secluded, heavily treed lot of the condominium unit we saw set the mood. Well furnished and decorated, it offered lovely, serene and private views from its many spacious windows. Just the place to kick back and relax in the whirlpool or in front of the fireplace after an exhausting day of skiing, hiking, biking, golfing or visiting nearby Petoskey or Harbor Springs. Many fine restaurants, beaches and marinas are minutes away!

Condo units range in size from 1 bedroom/1 bath (sleep 2-4) to 3+ bedrooms/ 3 baths (sleep 10-12). All feature whirlpool spa, fireplace, deluxe kitchen with dishwasher and microwave, cable TV, telephone, washer and dryer. Linens and firewood are provided. Air con-

Open, contemporary interiors

ditioned units are available. Weekend rentals begin at approximately $260 (summer season) and $440 (ski season). Five and seven night specials range from $440 to $1834. (Special pricing discounts available during spring and fall seasons).

MICHIGAN COTTAGES • CHALETS • CONDOS • B&B'S

HAMLET VILLAGE (continued...)

We did not have an opportunity of visiting their resort homes (located between Boyne Highlands and Nubs Nob). However, we understand they range in size from chalet-style (1 bath, sleeps 6) to larger homes (3 bath, sleeps 10). The homes feature fireplace, complete kitchens, televisions and telephones. Some resort homes furnish linens, others require you bring your own. Weekend home rentals begin at approximately $240 (summer season) to $890 with five to seven night "specials" ranging from $350 to $1,603.

A 50% non-refundable advance reservation deposit is required. Rental deposit will be returned if your reserved unit can be re-rented. All units are no smoking. Pets and snowmobiles are not allowed. Cash, check, money order, Visa or Mastercard accepted. Open year around.

Rentals are available through Land Masters, Inc. at (616) 526-2641.

TROUT CREEK CONDOMINIUMS
HARBOR SPRINGS (REGION 5)
(616) 526-2148 OR (800) 678-3923

This year around condominium resort, set on open spacious grounds, was built less than 10 years ago and has gained a reputation for adult and family comfort, relaxation and fun!

Trout Creek features many diverse activities for its guests which include special children's programs, three pools, two Jacuzzis, one sauna PLUS tennis, basketball, volleyball courts and a well-stocked trout pond. Horseshoes, nature

Landscaped grounds at Trout Creek

and cross country ski trails and a party room/conference center are yet additional features. To top it off, their fitness training room offers a professional trainer and masseuse — there's even a tennis pro on staff!

The owners and operators at Trout Creek continue to investigate new activities and programs to entice guests including special children's activities and adult focused diet/health training programs.

Exceptional golfing and skiing are nearby. Special golf discounts available at area courses including Boyne and Little Traverse Bay. Ski discounts also

TROUT CREEK (continued...)

available at Nubs Nob and Boyne Highlands. While there's no direct lake or water access at Trout Creek, marinas and beaches are available at nearby Crooked Lake.

We were able to visit several units. All were maintained in excellent condition and were comfortable. Views varied from well groomed, land-scaped grounds to naturally wooded scenes and open grassy fields. Sizes ranged from one to three bedrooms containing single to king size beds with a contemporary country decor running

Well maintained, contemorary interiors

through most. Additional features included fireplaces, cable TV, and fully equipped kitchens with microwaves and dishwashers, some had fans and air conditioning. The three bedroom w/loft condominium unit had an inviting two person Jacuzzi tub in the master bedroom.

For active families or those seeking that special get away — there's some-thing for everyone at Trout Creek. Approx. 120 units available. Daily rates begin at $70, weekend packages begin at $200 and weekly rentals from $750. No pets permitted, though pet boarding facilities are nearby.

TORCHLIGHT RESORT
ROBERT & GLENDA KNOTT
TORCH LAKE (REGION 5)

(616) 544-8263

For the past seven years, Bob and Glenda Knott have welcomed and made comfortable visitors to their friendly Torchlight Resort. Since Bob's retirement from GM, he and Glenda have devoted full time to their resort which features six lakeview cottages ranging in size. Their open, gently sloping grounds rest on the banks of

Aerial View of Torchlight

19

MICHIGAN COTTAGES • CHALETS • CONDOS • B&B'S

TORCHLIGHT (continued...)

Torch Lake with a pier large enough to dock a 30 ft. boat...so, if you've got one, bring it along! There's great fishing for northern pike, jumbo perch, bass, brown trout, musky, steelhead, to name a few. Their beach is safe for swimming and there's a playground for children.

All cottages offer lake views

We had the opportunity of visiting all six cottages and were pleased with their very clean, well maintained, and very comfortable interiors. Each was fully carpeted with private baths, full beds and queen size sleeper sofas. Kitchens featured new stoves and refrigerators. All had a lake view.

Their largest cottage sits closest to the water and was our favorite! Spacious with a terrific view of the Lake from its large picture window, it had an airy, open kitchen and living area with lovely furniture and attractive window treatments.

A very comfortable, down-to-earth get away can be found here at Torchlight Resort, and at prices that are very affordable! Weekly rental

Interior of larger cottage

rates begin at $300 with nightly rates beginning at $45. No pets. 10% senior citizens discounts offered. Open spring-fall.

RIVERS EDGE/LAKESIDE/SLEEPY HOLLOW
BOB & BETTY KACZMAREK, OWNERS
CENTRAL LAKE (REGION 5)
(810) 363-8814

We were very impressed with the overall cleanliness, comfort and quality of renovations completed and/or in progress at the Kaczmarek's three cozy, waterfront cottages.

All three cottages have two bedrooms (full and bunk beds) plus queen size sofa sleeper in living area. Kitchens are fully equipped including microwave,

RIVER'S EDGE, LAKESIDE, SLEEPY HOLLOW (continued...)

popcorn poppers (Bob loves popcorn!), utensils, dishes, color TV and VCR. Also included are picnic tables, gas grills and use of a rowboat and/or pontoon boat.

The first of the properties is *River's Edge*. Set back from the road, it sits very close to the river on the Chain-of-Lakes waterway. Secluded and quiet, this was our favorite! The clean, log interior was very cozy with new sleeper sofa and carpeting. Also new here is the kitchen with attractive countertops, sink and appliances. Plus, our favorite, the newly renovated screened porch with sparkling white ceramic tiled floor and an unhampered, relaxing view of the water.

River's Edge **Cottage**

The small bathroom was still under-going renovation but already included a new shower/tub stall. The double beds had newer mattresses and were very comfortable.

Interior of *Lakeside*

The second and third cottages are *Lakeside* and *Sleepy Hollow*. These log constructed lodgings, set back from the road on nicely treed grounds, and directly overlook the lake. Located on the same property, each feature warm knotty pine interiors, newer kitchens, appliances and furnishings. Sitting/living areas were cozy and comfortable. At the time we visited their small bathrooms, while fully functional, were in the process of renovation. The first bedroom in each contained a very comfortable double bed. The second bedrooms were much smaller, even bunk beds seemed tight. However, the new queen size sofa sleeper in the living area looked comfortable! Both properties had screened porches—these also are on Bob's list for updating.

Here are three comfortable lodgings in quiet settings for your private family getaway! Affordably priced at $400 to $450 per week. *River's Edge* is available for year around rental.

MICHIGAN COTTAGES • CHALETS • CONDOS • B&B'S

PRIVATE COTTAGE
WEST BAY, TRAVERSE CITY (REGION 5)
(616) 947-5948

This one bedroom (two full beds), beach house is only three blocks from downtown Traverse City, 1 block to tennis courts. Smaller but delightful, this beach house offers a very comfortable, cozy getaway!

Scenic setting offering great sunset view

The cottage sits several hundred feet behind the owner's home on a serene, private treed lot. Its expanse of large picture windows directly overlooks Grand Traverse Bay (what a view — what sunsets!). Interior furnishings are newer, attractive, appeared comfortable and include cable TV. The bright, cheery kitchen (fully equipped including microwave) is very clean and appealing with lovely corner windows offering a view of natural trees, lawn and shrubbery. The small bathroom area features glass stall shower (provide your own linens). Use of rowboat and canoe are included in the rental price. Available for summer rentals. Reasonably priced ($700 weekly), this one is a gem!

RICH & JANE CARLSON
TORCH LAKE (REGION 5)
(513) 579-0473

This spacious (3 bedroom, 2 bath) brick, ranch style home sits on one acre of land with 100 feet of Torch Lake frontage. Set high and back from the water on well groomed and landscaped grounds, 24 stairs takes you to lower grounds and water's edge. The lake is safe for swimming but does have a stony

22

CARLSON HOME (continued...)

bottom—so be sure to bring along your aqua shoes! There's also a dock available for your boat.

Traditionally furnished, the home's interior is very clean, comfortable and well maintained. The L-shaped dining/living area is open with large windows offering a view of sloping grounds and lake. The spacious kitchen is fully equipped including all appliances, dishwasher, coffee maker and microwave. Bedrooms are nicely decorated with very comfortable beds (twin beds, full

Traditionally furnished interior

bed and queen size beds). Additional features include fireplace, three color TVs with remote controls, washer/dryer, and two-car garage with remote door opener. The sunroom is bright and airy and leads you to a large, open wooden deck with picnic table and gas grill. Truly all the comforts of home!

There is no air conditioning. However, the cool breeze from Torch Lake usually does a great job of keeping things comfortable for all but the hottest days.

It is available for rental March-August. Weekly rentals only. All rental money required up front. Ask about refund policy. Please book as far in advance as possible! No pets/no smoking. Rents weekly for $1,200 during prime summer season.

A COUNTRY PLACE COTTAGES & BED & BREAKFAST, ART & LEE NIFFENEGGER SOUTH HAVEN (REGION 6)
(616) 637-5523

Warm, charming, comfortable and inviting best describe A Country Place Cottages and Bed & Breakfast! One of our greatest "finds" during our recent review tours!

The most delightful feature of each of the Niffenegger's three cottages is the bright pine interiors and restored wooden floors — so clean and shiny you can almost see your reflection! Most unique are the decorative touches to the cottage interiors which add to their warmth and charm—something usually found in a bed and breakfasts but seldom cottages. There are bright curtains,

23

MICHIGAN COTTAGES • CHALETS • CONDOS • B&B'S

A Country Place (continued...)

The Belvedere - 1 of 3 cottages

hand made quilts and other handcrafted decorations which clearly demonstrates the Niffenegger's wish to make you feel welcomed and your stay enjoyable. The kitchens are fully equipped including microwave, stove, etc.

The two cottages with direct beach access are *The Belvedere* and *The Retreat. The Belvedere*

is in front of Th*e Retreat* and is the larger of the two with three bedrooms (two queen beds and two twin beds). Additional features are high vaulted ceiling, ceiling fans, TV, and spacious deck. Somewhat smaller but offering the best sunset from its deck is *The Retreat.* Its single bedroom contains one double and one queen bed. TV, ceiling fan and private deck are also featured. (Guests to *The Retreat* should take note, the bathroom is in two parts. Toilet and sink are in one small room with the shower stall in a small sliding door area off the bedroom).

Beach Accessed through private stairway

The third cottage, The *Cottage*, is located on the same premises as the bed and breakfast. This one room (plus loft) country charm cottage features an inviting king size bed on the main floor with two twin beds in the loft. A private bath and shower are down the short hallway. To add to the coziness of the main room, there's a wood burning Franklin stove, full kitchen and sitting area with TV.

Sleeping area of *The Cottage*

Again, its country decorations, fresh pine and restored wood floors make for a warm, friendly interior. The enclosed wicker furnished front porch offers a view of the bed and breakfast backyard gardens, screened gazebo and lawn. The back deck is private with wooded view.

For those whose interests lean toward the friendly warmth of a

A Country Place (continued...)

bed and breakfast, Lee and Art (along with their friendly white and gray cat, Munchkin) welcome you to their century old, Greek Revival home situated on five acres of woodland (beach access to Lake Michigan 1/2 block away). You'll find an English oak and country theme throughout with carpeting and wall covering in shades of dusty rose or blues in their five rooms — touches of lace, accents of floral prints, antique furnishings and other small treasures. All rooms offer private bath, double or queen size beds, ceiling fans

A Country Place Bed & Breakfast

and air conditioning. Their *Windsor Room* (the only guest room located on the first floor) features a king size bed and bath with jet tub. Guests to their bed and breakfast enjoy a full breakfast of home baked goodies served in the formal dining area or, weather permitting, spacious deck or enclosed porch.

Cottages rent for about $450 to $700 (weekly) and $75 to $100 (daily), are open May through October and are great for private getaways or family fun. Their bed and breakfast is available year around and caters to both business and adult vacation travelers. Room rentals range from $50 to $85 daily. No smoking/ pets. $50 advance deposit required.

ARUNDEL HOUSE, AN ENGLISH B&B
Pat & Tom Zapal, South Haven (Region 6)
(616) 637-4790

Having moved to America many years ago from England and now a long-time resident of South Haven, Pat and Tom maintain this lovely bed and breakfast in a style of true charming English tradition. Pat definitely likes to spend time with her guests, to create new friends

Arundel, reminiscent of earlier times

MICHIGAN COTTAGES • CHALETS • CONDOS • B&B'S

ARUNDEL (continued...)

and cater to their needs and comforts. Most of Pat's guests come back year after year — to relax at the beaches, sail in the waters, and visit with their good friends, Pat and Tom. This turn-of-the-century home built in 1898 and moved

to its current location in 1905, has been fully restored to its original beauty and charm and is registered with the Michigan Historical Society. Arundel's styling is reminiscent of the days when seagoing ships sailed the Great Lakes. Sitting room and small library as well as each of their guest rooms are decorated in Victorian style with lace, antiques and authentic reproductions. The eight guest rooms (with shared and private baths) are cheery and bright, highlighted in shades of blues, pink, white and charcoal. Special touches in each antique-filled room include crochet throws and marble topped dressers.

Victorian styled rooms

Continental buffet breakfasts are served daily and on special occasions, afternoon tea with freshly prepared scones (Pat prides herself on her scones!) and cucumber sandwiches. Several guests we "secretly" spoke to gave us their high praises of the owners and of their wonderful and memorable stays at Arundel.

Located a very short distances to beach, restaurants, shops and marina. Open year around. Daily rates range from $50-$80.

SLEEPY HOLLOW RESORT
SOUTH HAVEN (REGION 6)
(616) 637-1127

This traditional resort, built 58 years ago in Art Deco style, has been operated by its current owner for 22 years. With large, open, naturally treed and attractively landscaped grounds, it is one of the few remaining resorts which still caters to the "all-in-one" family vacation. This happens to be Sleep Hollow's greatest feature! There's a "live" theater, restaurant/lodge, tennis courts, Olympic size pool and several children's play areas scattered throughout the grounds (their beach is accessed through a steep series of stairs).

Some of the special features at Sleep Hollow include:

Ichabod's Restaurant. Located in the lodge, this wood paneled and country themed restaurant offers its diners a warm, down-home atmosphere and serves up tasty meals. There are special evening family cook-outs and Sunday Brunches with weekends featuring "theme" meals which attract both resort guests and outside visitors alike.

Icabonds & lodge scenic setting

Legend Theatre. Set in a bright red barn, the theatre with auditorium style seating offers plays, music and other

live entertainment once or twice a week with laser-disc movies shown on 40" screen TV off days. The atmosphere here is down-home and definitely creates the mood for relaxation and nighttime enjoyment.

Entertainment at the *Legend Theatre*

Children's Program. For adults who may wish to enjoy some "free time", there are super-vised children's activities morning, afternoons and some evenings (children four and over). Children will also enjoy the many play areas scattered throughout the grounds.

Numerous cottages wind throughout the wooded grounds, each of varying sizes (1-3 bedrooms). Also available to guests are hotel units and apart-ments. The large apartment building rests on spacious grounds and over-looks the water near the tree covered ridge (many apartments offer "peek-a-boo" views of the lake between the tall trees).

Unfortunately for us, Sleepy Hollow was very busy at that time we visited (early June). We were only able to view efficiency and joined apartment units. We would have liked to have seen some of the larger cottages to gain a better impression of overall accommodations — perhaps next time. Interiors of the lodgings we visited were clean with functional

Simple unit interiors

27

MICHIGAN COTTAGES • CHALETS • CONDOS • B&B'S

SLEEPY HOLLOW (continued...)

furnishings (daybed sofas, folding tables and plastic molded chairs). Kitchens were fully equipped and bathrooms in good repair. The lodgings we visited did not offer exceptional comfort — but with so many things to do at Sleepy Hollow, who has time to spend inside?

Rates for 2-day weekends range from $130 to $310 with week-long stays during prime season (June 26-September 4) ranging from $450 to $1,040. No pets. Open seasonal.

OAK COVE RESORT
BOB & SUSAN WOJCIK
LAWRENCE (REGION 6)
(616) 674-8228

Oak Cove Resort (built in 1910) rests among 15 acres of wooded land along 500 ft. of beautiful, spring-fed Lake Cora. You won't find telephones, TV's or fancy suites at Oak Cove, but you will find plenty of family fun and down-home warmth from its owners, Bob and Susan Wojcik. They're always there with a friendly smile, a fresh pot of coffee or a quiet chat.

Scenic views from dining room & lodge

We've been told some of the best local fish stories come from Bob. Susan's culinary talents at preparing delicious, hearty yet well balanced meals for guests in this American Plan (all meals provided) resort are well known. Having visited the picturesque setting of Oak Cove Resort, it's understandable why it was rated as "One of the Midwest's Best Cottage Resorts" in the April 1994 issue of *Midwest Living* magazine.

While there are no "planned" activities here, there's plenty to do. This includes water volley ball, shuffleboard, heated swimming pool, baseball diamond, chip shot practice area, beach and excellent fishing (Susan says she's happy to cook any fish you catch...as long as you do the cleaning!). Rowboats, canoes and paddleboats are always available for guests' use. There's also a walking/ nature trail and the whole family can enjoy the "Fun House" cottage with video games, pool table, small library and sitting area with tables. And for

OAK COVE (continued...)

you golfing enthusiasts, Oak Cove's very moderate rates also include use of the nearby golf course (Bob & Susan will provide babysitters, at guest's expense, if requested).

The lodgings consist of 10, very clean, one to five bedroom cottages and seven lodge rooms. The smaller cottages sit closest to the water with some directly overlooking the lake. Most cottages are styled more like sleeping rooms with private baths/showers, no kitchens and minimal or no interior sitting areas. Three units located at the

Cottages with lake view

front of the lot (closest to the road) are larger home-like units (the largest being 1,600 sq. ft.) and include equipped kitchens, large living areas, fireplaces and air conditioning, with up to five bedrooms (sleep up to 10).

For couples or individuals, the lodge offers seven upstairs sleeping rooms (some with king and queen size beds) which share 4 baths (the lodge is a smoke-free environment). These cozy, inviting rooms offer air conditioning and comfortable mattresses. You'll enjoy the lovely views from the Lodge rooms which overlook the lake or wooded grounds.

Also, at the lodge is the Wojcik's charming, antique filled dining area with an excellent view of the lake. Breakfast, lunch and dinner, freshly prepared in Susan's own special style, are served daily. And, while here, be sure to visit the Museum Room which Susan decorates with antique clothing and collectibles from the 1800's as well as mementos from the Wojcik's own early history.

At the time of this writing, weekly rates, per person, were: $295 (lodge rooms); $315 per week, per adult (for cabins, assumes 6 nights); daily rates $85 for a single or $135 per couple. This, of course, includes all meals, all resort ammenities and one round of golf per day, per adult.

Interior of lake view cottage

Senior citizen outings and "Ladies Only" Spa weeks are offered during special weekends throughout the summer. Currently open end of May to September...Susan may decide to remain open year around for cross country skiing and great ice fishing...call to confirm. No pets.

MICHILINDA BEACH LODGE
WHITEHALL (REGION 6)

(616) 893-1895

Spacious, well maintained natural grounds with bright annuals and perennials in decorative display are the first things to greet visitors to Michilinda. This Modified American Plan resort (breakfasts and dinners are included in price - lunches are provided at additional cost) rests on the shores of Lake Michigan and has been in operation almost 60 years. Don Eilers, the current manager, has been running the resort for almost 25 of those years.

Well maintained grounds & lodging

Michilinda provides every opportunity for couples or families to keep their days fun filled. There's the heated swimming and wading pools, kids playground, tennis courts, shuffleboard, basket-ball, volley ball, tether ball, mini-golf area and beach (beach size varies depending on Lake Michigan—at the time we visited it was almost nonexistent). Horseback riding, trips to the sand dunes or a visit to one of Michigan's largest amusement and water parks is not far away. There's also special activities taking place each week including Western Campfire Night, Staff Variety Shows, supervised children's activities (ages 3-9); Tournaments (informal tennis and shuffleboard); Tee Off Golf Outings, Bingo and more!

The historic main lodge (The Holiday House), built in 1904, is well maintained with cozy country decor and stained/leaded glass doors at its entrance. A spacious sitting area contains sofas, chairs, fireplace with dining area overlooking Lake Michigan. The lodge also contains a small gift shop and TV room with guest rooms on the upper floors.

Many units have lake views

MICHILINDA (continued...)

All rooms offer private baths. This includes accommodations at both the main lodge and 10 other buildings. Most rooms have two beds (twin or double). Others feature multiple bedroom suites and separated sitting rooms or sitting areas. Several rooms have lake views and offer balconies or decks. Others sit away from the lake breezes and are equipped with air conditioners (several are handicap accessible).

We were able to visit several lodge rooms and were very impressed with the cleanliness, comfort and lovely views from each (a series of stairs takes you to all lodge rooms). We found each to offer its own unique "look" of warmth with knotty pine interiors, country wallpaper, "grandma's attic" type ceilings or studio ceilings. Bathrooms were well maintained with sparkling sinks and countertops. Beds were covered with bright and cheery spreads and comfortably firm mattresses.

Because a large family reunion was filling all standard and deluxe cottage and chalet units, we were only able to visit an economy duplex unit. The main living area of this simply furnished unit contained sofa and chair but no kitchen or tables. The high cathedral ceiling in both this room and the master bedrooms added an appealing open/airy feeling. Wallpaper and paneling were in good condition. The front bedroom's double bed was very comfortable as was the units second bedroom which contained two twin beds with

Comfortable bedroom of duplex

doorwall. The bathroom, again, was very clean with separated sink and toilet/bath areas.

Daily room rates at Michilinda range from $130 to $161 with weekly rates ranging from $680 to $1,025. Cottage rentals begin at $210 (daily) to $1,075-$1,310 (weekly). Children's daily rates are $33 with weekly rates ranging from $170 to $300 (children 3 and under free). All rates assume two people and include breakfast and dinner. There is a charge for each additional person. Michilinda is open May through early October. No Pets.

DOUBLE JJ RESORT
ROTHBURY (REGION 6)

(616) 894-4444

As you drive along the roadway leading to Double JJ Resort, you'll pass beautifully manicured grounds, green pastures, wooded hills, archery and rifle ranges, and numerous horseback riders making their way to trails. There's no question that you're about to begin an adventure! You're here to truly unwind and enjoy a unique and exciting time. Here, in the far west side of central Michigan is our own, genuine, 1,000 acre western ranch-style getaway!

This American Plan ranch resort (all meals included) caters to adult couples, groups and singles who want to enjoy group, outdoor activities and have a great time (sorry, children are not permitted on The Ranch grounds).

Western styling at The Ranch

Of course, the main feature here is the excellent horseback riding. Maintaining and breeding their own stock of over 60 horses, Double JJ assures their animals are kept healthy, happy and well trained. For first time riders or pros, they'll have the horse and trail just right for you! And, if you'd like to really learn how to ride (not just sit on the saddle) or improve your riding, the resort staffs professional instructors who will train you in both English and Western style riding. There are always plenty of professional wranglers at Double JJ to help out!

And for you golfing enthusiasts, there's the championship, 18-hole Thoroughbred Golf Course. Designed by nationally renowned golf course architect, Arthur Hill. It is rated as the 10th most challenging course in the nation. Of course, it is also enjoyed by beginner and intermediate golfers alike. There's a pro shop here with bar and grill, practice chipping and putting greens, driving range, daily clinics and private lessons.

Championship Golf Course

The fun doesn't stop with the excellent horses and exceptional golf, however! There's plenty of other things to do, including archery and rifle ranges, heated

32

DOUBLE JJ (CONTINUED...)

pool, hot tub, volleyball or shuffleboard. Or, if you prefer, take one of their paddleboats, canoes or row boats and explore the two surrounding lakes.

Evenings are filled with dancing in their atmospheric barn-styled lounge featuring variety of nightly entertainment. There's hayrides, BBQs on the beach, night-owl sing-a-longs, all-night volleyball, Staff Shows, and every Friday night "The Rodeo".

Sleeping room at *The Ranch*

Lodging are of two distinct types at Double JJ — *Ranch* accommodations (located in the hub of activities) and the newer *Thoroughbred* accommodations (on the grounds of the golf course). Lodgings at the *Ranch* have been around for almost 60 years and are adult-exclusive. There's a quaint, old-time western look here—from authentic bunk-house atmosphere to

New *Thoroughbred* Hotel/Condos

rustic cabin/sleeping rooms. Lodgings at the *Ranch* are small and spartan but clean and comfortable with rooms sleeping from two to seven people (double, twin or bunk beds). Deluxe rooms feature queen beds, mini-refrigerators and coffeemakers. All have private baths. Atmosphere at the *Ranch* is very relaxed. No one even locks their doors!

These rooms are definitely for people who want to be in the hub of all the action — who only plan on using their room to catch a few hours of sleep before moving on to the next activity.

For individuals requiring more quiet time, prefer a more luxurious surrounding, are more interested in golf, or wish to bring their children, the newly built (1994) *The Thoroughbred* hotel/condominium accommodations would be your choice. Set along the scenic golf course and 40 acre lake, the hotel/condos are a short drive to the *Ranch*. Exterior design maintains the country image with natural wood and contemporary

Standard Room at the *Thoroughbred*

MICHIGAN COTTAGES • CHALETS • CONDOS • B&B'S

DOUBLE JJ (continued...)

decorations. Hotel rooms feature cable TV, air conditioning with standard to luxury accommodations (multi-room suites offering king size beds, Jacuzzis and more). Condominiums are one and two bedrooms with lofts and include full kitchens, dishwashers, microwave, Jacuzzi, fireplace, king-size beds and private decks.

Currently open May 1 to November 1. Hotel and condominium may remain open longer. Contact Double JJ to confirm. Rates at the *Ranch* lodges range from weekends ($209 to $229) to weekly ($644 to $714). Rates at the *Thoroughbred* range weekends from $229 to $259 (hotel) to $279 (condo); weekly rates $609 to $689 (hotel) to $889 (condo). Rates per person based on maximum room occupancy. Double JJ offers various rate specials including daily and mini-vacation packages.

YELTON MANOR BED & BREAKFAST
ELAINE HERBERT & ROB KRIPAITIS
SOUTH HAVEN (REGION 6)
(616) 637-5220

If you're tired of 60 hour work weeks, too many business meetings, eating on the run and the daily pressures of today's lifestyle, Yelton's is the place to go. Elaine Herbert and Rob Kripaitis are former corporate professionals who decided to step back several years ago to a more leisurely lifestyle. They have developed Yelton's to cater and pamper their guests for a truly luxurious get-a-way.

Yelton's actually consists of two buildings. Both are decorated in contemporary luxury with deep blue, dark green, and dust rose carpeting throughout, floral and stripped wallpapers and dark rich woods.

In the main house, the rooms are light and airy, the beds piled high with pillows and many rooms have Jacuzzi's. Down-

Yelton's impressive exterior & grounds

stairs you'll find a cozy living room, elegant dining room and their entertainment room with fireplace, TV, VCR (they have a

34

YELTONS (continued...)

large video library) and game table. There is also a small bar area where there is always fresh popcorn to go along with your favorite beverage.

In the morning a full, rich breakfast is served, exquisitely prepared by their cook. These breakfasts are not "heart smart". As Elaine explained, people watch their diets and try to eat right all year long. When they come here to be

pampered, they want foods they don't normally get. That probably explains why you will find an assortment of candies and pastries throughout the main house all day long for your enjoyment. There are also hors d'oeuvres usually served in the evening.

Elegantly maintained and inviting guest room

The adjacent building is designed for those people who truly want to get away. The rooms and suites are larger, most with jacuzzi and fireplace. The first floor suite is handicap accessible. For the people staying in this building, breakfast is served at your door, if you prefer. Ideal for that *special*, romantic getaway!

The outside of the property is perfectly landscaped with a small gazebo and several areas to sit and relax during the day or evening as you watch the sunset over Lake Michigan. Yeltons is directly across the street from the lake and within walking distance to the center of the city. South Haven has some great shops, restaurants and plenty to see and do. No smoking/pets.

Relaxing sitting rooms

Yelton's is, without question, a premiere bed and breakfast. Prices range from about $90 to $170.

THE SILVERBEACH FUNHOUSE
HOWARD & KELLY ADAMS
ST. JOSEPH (REGION 6)
(616) 983-2959

Fun and energy best describe Howard and Kelly Adams, owners of the Silverbeach Funhouse. They love St. Joseph and its history and I spent an enjoyable afternoon listening to Kelly tell me all about it.

Brightly painted - The *Funhouse*

The two story, bright yellow house gets its name from the past. In the late 1800's, Silver Beach had an amusement park called the Funhouse. It was known for two special rides ... The Saucer and The Cup. They have decorated the home to reflect the mood of that funhouse. There are sea shells, fishing nets, early 1900's bathing suits and similar memorabilia on the walls. You will find comfortable casual furniture, inflatable palm trees and other funhouse decor. A unique way to decorate a home and Kelly has done a great job with it!

Kicky and *fun* interior stylings

The first floor (*Saucer*) is large and holds up to 10 people with two large bedrooms, bath and fully equipped kitchen. The second floor (*Cup*) is smaller to accommodate six with one large bedroom, bath and kitchen. The yard has a picnic table and grill for the family to enjoy.

Directly across the street is the bright silver beach resting against the deep blue of Lake Michigan. The city has restored the beach and you will find a large play area for children, refreshment stands, and plenty of sand to relax on. While here you can learn to wind surf, boogie board or skin board. Near by there is tennis, golf, shopping and more. St. Joseph has some excellent restaurants that Kelly and Howard would be happy to tell you about. In the summer, just a block from the Funhouse the city offers free concerts and wagon rides.

St. Joseph is a city for fun and so is the Funhouse. The Adams are working on restoring two more homes right next to the Funhouse which should be complete by 1995. A great place for the family, the *Saucer* rents for $800 a week and the *Cup* $550.

36

THE VICTORIA RESORT
BOB AND JAN, SOUTH HAVEN (REGION 6)
(616) 637-6414

Just a block or two from Lake Michigan, this three acre resort specializes in family entertainment. The large well groomed front lawn is ideal for relaxing or outdoor games. Also available is the outdoor pool, well main-

tained tennis and basket-
ball courts, volleyball,
horse shoes, playground
and lots and lots of bikes
for the family. Most eve-
nings you'll find the
guests sitting around the
portable outdoor fireplace
relaxing after a hard day
of fun. In the next year or
two Bob and Jan plan on
adding a gazebo and
cobblestone walks, which
will make a nice touch.

Victoria Resort's apartments — well maintained grounds & lodging

Four cottages available

The resort consists of four cottages, the apartment style resort building and the main building where breakfast is served. The main building is beautiful and rich with dark woods, thick carpeting, and crystal chandeliers and is reminiscent of the turn-of-the-century. A full breakfast is served at the formal dining room table each morning for those living in the apartments.

The apartments are very nice ranging from small and cozy rooms to large and elegant suites. They all have private baths, air conditioning and/or ceiling fans. Their suites also feature whirlpool tubs. The lobby, or living area has cable TV and a fireplace, for those cool evenings. They plan on renovating and enlarging a couple of the smaller rooms to create another suite.

The cottages are off to one side and though we could not see the interiors (they were occupied) the units looked very well maintained. These two and three bedroom cottages come with daily maid service. The hotel units range from $60 to $100 daily, weekends slightly higher. Cottage rates are $750 and $900 a week.

37

REGION 1

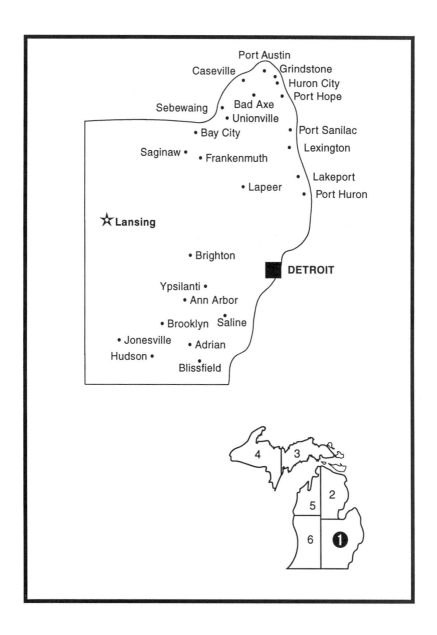

Port Austin
Caseville
Grindstone
Huron City
Port Hope
Sebewaing
Bad Axe
Unionville
Bay City
Port Sanilac
Saginaw •
Lexington
• Frankenmuth
Lakeport
• Lapeer
Port Huron
☆ Lansing
• Brighton
■ DETROIT
Ypsilanti •
• Ann Arbor
• Brooklyn Saline
• Jonesville • Adrian
Hudson •
Blissfield

REGION 1

Entering the southeast side of Michigan is the Heartland, the only area in Michigan without links to the Great Lakes. Here, too, the territory is agricultural with faded red barns and rolling fields of oats. As you travel along, you will see gentle hills and vails of lush green as far as your eye can see. Crystal lakes, rippling streams, waterfalls, hot air balloon races, air shows and many tours of historic homes, art fairs, unusual shops and stagecoach towns of long ago. Vibrant cities that never seem to sleep. Its treasure lies in the scenic beauty of its woods, lakes and streams made even more beautiful by the fine people and relaxed atmosphere of the area.

Shaped by the Saginaw Bay to the west and Lake Huron to the east, the "Thumb" is a world apart from the urban communities that are less than two hours away. For here the interstate highways turn to country roads and the suburbs turn into distinct villages, the hectic life of the city turns into rural country charm. There are 90 miles of lake shorelines to view, small museums, beaches, country markets, antique shops, roadside parks, and picturesque bluffs, lighthouses, and an easy way of life to soothe the soul and rest the weary urban mind.

Welcome to "the gateway close to home".

ADRIAN • IRISH HILLS AREA

COVERS: BLISSFIELD • BROOKLYN • HUDSON • JONESVILLE

Adrian, a unique blend of modern and historic! Visit the Croswell Opera House, the oldest continuously operated theater of its kind in Michigan! It features live theater productions as well as special art exhibits. Michigan Futurity is the place to be for horse racing excitement.

Surround yourself by the beauty of the **Irish Hills**! Picnic by one of the area's 50 spring-fed lakes, ride amongst its beautiful rolling hills, and take a trip to historic Walker Tavern in Cambridge State Historic Park. Enjoy a nature walk through the 670-acre Hidden Lake Gardens at Michigan State University. Of course, there's always the fun of Mystery Hill. Ready for more? Then step back in time to the 1800's and enjoy the pioneering spirit that lives on at Stagecoach Stop U.S.A. Sit back with a sarsaparilla in the Saloon, pan for gold, or take a train ride ... but be careful ... we hear there's masked bandits in the area!

Join the excitement of Indy and stock car races each summer (June-August) at the Michigan International Speedway in the Irish Hills. While enjoying the beautiful fall colors, don't forget to stop in **Brooklyn** and join the fun at Oktoberfest or their arts and crafts festival. Anyone for cross-country skiing or snowmobiling? Cambridge State Historic Park is waiting. No matter what time of year, the Irish Hills are always waiting.

For additional information on special events in the area, contact:

Brooklyn/Irish Hills Chamber of Commerce
P.O. Box 405
Brooklyn, MI 49230
(517) 592-8907

ADRIAN

BRIAROAKS INN   **(517) 263-1659**
CONNIE & DALLAS MARVIN   **BED & BREAKFAST**
Set among century old oak trees, overlooking Beaver Creek, this charming, completely renovated Williamsburg style inn awaits its guests. Features private baths, A/C, TV and phones. Their special guest room features canopy bed, whirlpool for two and breakfast in your room. 3 rooms.

Daily $65-$125

BLISSFIELD

HIRAM D. ELLIS INN   **(517) 486-3155**
              BED & BREAKFAST

All rooms in this 1880's, 2-story brick Victorian inn offer phones, CATV, private baths, and complimentary use of bicycles. Come, relax and enjoy the many antiques and specialty shops in the area! Continental breakfast served each morning. 4 rooms.

Daily $50-$70

BROOKLYN
(IN THE HEART OF THE IRISH HILLS)

CHICAGO STREET INN **(800) 252-5674 • (517) 592-3888**
KAREN & BILL KERR   **BED & BREAKFAST**

Antique furnishings, original electric chandeliers, European stained glass windows, and a wicker filled veranda decorate this 1800's Queen Anne Victorian home. Wonderful full breakfasts featuring homemade baked good are unexpected treats! Minutes from numerous lakes, golfing, hiking, antiquing. 3 suites with Jacuzzis and fireplaces. 7 rooms w/private baths, A/C.

Daily $75-$150

DEWEY LAKE MANOR   **(517) 467-7122**
THE PHILLIPS FAMILY   **BED & BREAKFAST**

Sitting atop a knoll overlooking Dewey Lake on 18 scenic acres, a "country retreat" awaits Manor guests! Picnic by the lake — enjoy evening bonfires. Hearty continental breakfasts are served on the glass enclosed porch (weather permitting). At night, snack on popcorn or sip a cup of cider...there are always cookies! 4 rooms w/private baths, A/C.

Daily $55-$65

KAREN KERR   **(517) 592-3888**
              COTTAGE

Located on Clark Lake this single lakefront cottage sleeps 4 to 6 people. Fully furnished with equipped kitchen, offers TV and A/C. No pets.

Call for Rates

DUANE LOCKE   **(313) 971-7558**
COTTAGE

Lakefront cottage on Wamples Lake sleeps up to 6. Features large enclosed porch, excellent swimming and fishing boat. No pets.

Weekly $450

JANET WITT   **(419) 878-7201**
COTTAGES

Two fully furnished cottages available with convenient lake access. Clean and comfortable home away from home. Fully equipped kitchen, color TV, VCR, picnic table, gas grill, boat with life jackets. Available weekly June-August.

Weekly $450

HUDSON

SUTTON'S-WEED FARM B&B   **(517) 547-6302 • (800)-826-FARM**
BED & BREAKFAST

You'll step back in time when you're a guest at this 7 gable Victorian farmhouse (built 1874) decorated with five generations of antiques. Stroll along the 170 acres of wooded trails and watch for the many deer and other wildlife. Breakfast to your taste—reservations, please. No, smoking. No pets. 4 rooms.

Daily $55-$65

JONESVILLE

THE MUNRO HOUSE   **(517) 849-9292**
JOYCE YARDE   **BED & BREAKFAST**

An elegant and inviting 1840 Greek Revival home has 10 fireplaces, 6 chandeliers, 12 ft. ceilings and a sweeping staircase. First brick home in Hillsdale County and served as an underground railroad station. Near Hillsdale College, golf, x-country skiing, theater, museum and antique shops. Coffee and desserts served in the evening. Five rooms with private baths, phones, TV.

Daily $45-$68

ANN ARBOR • BRIGHTON • SALINE • YPSILANTI

Ann Arbor, home of the University of Michigan. This cosmopolitan area offers year around activities for its visitors — from arts and crafts to live theater and entertainment. While here, be sure to stroll the many unique shops, visit the University of Michigan planetariums, canoe, swim or hike in Gallup Park. In late July, arts and craft enthusiasts never miss the Ann Arbor Art Fair featuring noted artisans from across the country. Only 10 miles from Ann Arbor rests **Saline.** Noted for its historic homes and antique shops, the area hosts nationally recognized antique shows from April through November. **Ypsilanti**, home of Eastern Michigan University, is also a city of diverse activities! Among its many points of interest include Wiard's Orchard which offers fresh cider, tours and hayrides and enjoy the festivities for its yearly Heritage Festival (celebrated each August) commenorating its early French settlers!

Surrounded by lakes, the **Brighton** area offers excellent golf courses, parks, downhill and cross country skiing. In the summer, Independence, Folk Art and Farmer's Market festivals abound at Mill Pond located in the heart of the city.

For additional information on events and activities, contact:

Ann Arbor CVB
211 E. Huron, Suite 6
Ann Arbor, MI 48104
(313) 995-7281

Greater Brighton Area Chamber
131 Hayne Street
Brighton, MI 48116
(800) 227-5086 • (517) 592-8907

ANN ARBOR

THE URBAN RETREAT BED & BREAKFAST — (313) 971-8110
BED & BREAKFAST

Contemporary ranch-styled home, antique furnished, set in a quiet neighborhood minutes from downtown and UM/EMU campuses. Adjacent to wildlife preserve, walking and jogging trails. A National Wildlife Federation "Backyard Wildlife Habitat". Full gourmet breakfasts. A/C. 2 rooms.

Daily $40-$60

BRIGHTON

BRIGHTON HOMES — (810) 227-3225
VACATION HOMES

This home, built in 1990, sleeps up to 8 and is completely furnished. Located in a secluded area, the balcony overlooks the water only 10 ft. away. Additional

BRIGHTON HOMES (continued...)
features include fully equipped kitchen with microwave, freezer, dishwasher, washer and dryer. Includes use of rowboat and dock.

Weekly   (summer) $600   (winter) $450

ISLAND LAKE RESORT   **(810) 229-6723**
ED & CHARLOTTE BAPRAWSKI   **COTTAGES**
With frontage on both Briggs and Island Lakes, the resort offers 1, 2 and 3 bedroom housekeeping cottages and duplex units. All lodgings are completely furnished and equipped (bring you own bed linens and towels). Use of boats are included. Beautiful sandy beach, playground, picnic tables, and more. 50% deposit required.

	1 Bedroom	Duplex	2 Bedroom	3 Bedroom
Weekly	$188	$278	$298	$328

SALINE

THE HOMESTEAD BED & BREAKFAST   **(313) 429-9625**
SHIRLEY GROSSMAN   **BED & BREAKFAST**
This 1851 circa brick farmhouse filled with period antiques, features comfort in Victorian elegance. Cross-country ski, stroll or simply relax on 50 acres of farmland. Only 10 minutes from Ann Arbor. A/C. Corporate rates available. 5 rooms.

Daily $30-$65

YPSILANTI

PARISH HOUSE INN   **(313) 480-4800**
                                                 BED & BREAKFAST
First constructed in 1893 by the First Congregational Church as a parsonage, this Queen Anne style home was extensively renovated in 1993. Charmingly decorated in Victorian style with period antiques. Fireplace, Jacuzzi, wet bar, CATV and telephones available. Gourmet breakfast. Dinner parties by reservation. No smoking. 9 rooms w/private baths.

Daily $65-$115

LANSING

Lansing, home of our State Capital since 1847. Visiting the Capital building is an absolute "must do" for visitors in the area. Guides conduct free tours daily! Also take some time to visit the Michigan Historical Museum and explore Michigan's dynamic and exciting past. Relax on a riverboat cruise on the Grand River. There's also plenty of excellent golfing, shops, galleries, live theater and restaurants. The Boars Head Theater (Michigan's only resident theater) and Woldumar Nature Center are additional attractions.

For additional information on events and activities, contact:

Greater Lansing CVB
119 Pere Marquette
Lansing, MI 48912
(800) 648-6630 • (517) 487-6800

LANSING

MAPLEWOOD BED & BREAKFAST	**(517) 372-7775**
PAT BUNCE	**BED & BREAKFAST**

Three acres of natural, scenic beauty greet visitors to this 1890 built B&B. Close to MSU and the State Capitol, Maplewood is located on the corner of Wood Road and State Road. Full breakfasts included. Major credit cards accepted. 3 rooms.

Daily $50-$60

WHEATFIELD HOUSE BED & BREAKFAST	**(517) 655-4327**
ROGER LANE GLUMM	**BED & BREAKFAST**

A massive house designed for relaxation and enjoyment. Wheatfield House features an indoor pool, hot tub and tanning booth, acres of woods for hiking, decks and balconies overlooking Deer Creek and the adjacent woods. Rooms range from modest to luxurious. Nearby Williamston hosts an impressive collection of antique dealers, restaurants and specialty shops.

Daily $55-$110

PORT HURON • LAKEPORT • LAPEER

Port Huron, where Lake Huron's waters become the St. Clair River. This port town is the home of the Blue Water Bridge, arts and craft fairs, waterfront dining and wonderful views from the shoreline. While in the area, visit Fort Gratiot Lighthouse and the Knowlton Ice Museum. In July, enjoy the excitement of the Blue Water Festival and the 3-day Port Huron to Mackinac Island Yacht Races.

Approximately 35 miles west of Port Huron, is the scenic countryside of **Lapeer**. Surrounded by orchards, the area is known for its blueberry farms. The many lakes and streams in the area offer good fishing. In the winter, enjoy one of Lapeer's groomed x-country ski trails.

For additional information on special events in the Port Huron area, contact:

Blue Water CVB
619 River Street, Port Huron, MI 48060
(810) 987-8687 • (800) 852-4242

LAKEPORT

HURON LAKE HOME   **(810) 364-4820**
PAUL MAYS   **HOME**
Located north of Lakeport State Park, this 3 bedroom (sleeps 8) brick bi-level house is approximately 1500 sq. ft. and offers a large yard and beach. Very private location, 50' x 70' lot, the home is completely furnished with fully equipped kitchen. Linens included (bring your own towels). Deck overlooks Lake Huron. Excellent swimming.

Weekly $650

LAPEER

HART HOUSE   **(810) 667-9106**
ELLIE HICKLING   **BED & BREAKFAST**
Listed on the National Historic Register, this delightful Queen Anne B&B was home of the first Mayor, Rodney G. Hart. Guests are served a full breakfast on weekends (continental weekdays) by a Victorian maid either in the dining room or at your door! Private baths. 3 rooms. No smoking.

Daily $30-$35

PORT HURON

THE VICTORIAN INN   **(810) 984-1437**
BED & BREAKFAST

This Queen Anne style Inn, authentically restored, offers its guests a timeless ambiance in one of its guest rooms—each uniquely decorated. Enjoy the Inn's classically creative cuisine and gracious service. One hour from Detroit. 4 rooms.

Daily $55-$65

LEXINGTON • PORT AUSTIN • CASEVILLE • BAD AXE

Covers: Grindstone • Huron City • Port Hope • Port Sanilac • Sebewaing • Unionville

K nown for its historic homes, **Lexington,** also offers excellent boating, fishing and swimming. Visit the general store (dating from the 1870's) and indulge in the tasty nostalgia of their "penny candy" counter. Walk to the marina and visit the old lighthouse (built in 1886).

Further north is **Port Hope**, home of the Bottom Land Preserve. The Lighthouse County Park, just outside town, is an ideal spot for scuba diving enthusiasts to view the under water wrecks of 19th century vessels.

Take the turn off to **Huron City,** and stroll among the historic recreations of a 19th Century village. Visit **Grindstone City** and see if you can spot some of the original grinding wheels made from sandstone. We understand the general store in Grindstone serves ice cream cones big enough to satisfy the hottest and hungriest of visitors.

Celebrate both outstanding sunrises and sunsets at the tip of the thumb in **Port Austin**. Stop at Finan's Drug Store's nostalgic soda fountain in the area's restored business district. Discover the rolling sand dunes hidden behind the trees at Port Crescent State Park. Relax on its excellent 3-mile beach. This is also a bird watcher's haven with abundant numbers of hawk, oriole, osprey and bluebird populations.

For a unique dining experience in Port Austin, try *The Bank* on Blake Street ... a little pricey, but worth it. This historic former bank is now an excellent restaurant, noted for its sourdough bread with herb butter and freshly prepared meals. Another excellent dining treat is offered at the *Garfield Inn* on Lake Street that serves as both a B&B and elegant restaurant. For more casual, relaxed dining you'll want to stop at the *Port Hope Hotel Restaurant* (in Port Hope). The hotel is no longer in operation, but we understand the restaurant is still preparing excellent hamburgers and other good, basic fare at affordable prices! Moving around

LEXINGTON • PORT AUSTIN • CASEVILLE • BAD AXE

(continued...)

the thumb is **Caseville**. Drive along its half-mile stretch of the Saginaw Bay Beach. Here's a great area for perch fishing, boating, swimming and just plain relaxing!

For additional information on special events in these areas, contact:

Huron County Economic Dev. Corp.
Huron County Bldg., Bad Axe, MI 48413
(800) 35-THUMB • (517) 269-6431

BAD AXE

THE CROSS HOUSE BED & BREAKFAST   **(517) 269-9466**
MARY SHUMAKER   **BED & BREAKFAST**

This bed and breakfast, located in town on 2-1/2 acres of land, features 6 impressively decorated rooms with AC and CATV. Fireside suite has canopy bed and natural fireplace and is perfect for weddings or special occasions. The Princess has king-size bed and whirlpool tub. Private baths are available. Open year around. Full breakfasts. Pet sitter available. MC /Visa accepted.

Rates $55-$95

CASEVILLE

BELLA VISTA MOTEL & COTTAGES   **(517) 856-2650**
                                    COTTAGES/EFFICIENCIES/MOTEL

In addition to their motel, this lodging offers 1 bedroom efficiencies with kitchenettes and 2 bedroom cottages with full kitchens. All cottages offer views of the water from their large picture windows and feature living room, screened porch and carports. Includes linens, tiled bath, electric heat, CATV w/HBO. Heated outdoor swimming pool, outside grills and picnic tables, large sun deck, shuffleboard courts, ping-pong, swings, 400 ft. of beach.

Daily $65-$85   Weekly $395-$625

COUNTRY CHARM FARM   **(517) 856-3110**
BOO DEPNER   **BED & BREAKFAST**

This antique filled B&B sits on 40 acres of land. Enjoy the fish stocked pond, deer, horses, ducks, rabbits, and cows on the premises. Continental breakfast served. Four rooms available offering both private and shared baths. No pets.

Daily $55-$65

MICHIGAN COTTAGES • CHALETS • CONDOS • B&B'S

CARKNER HOUSE   **(517) 856-3456**
                                               BED & BREAKFAST

Built around 1865, President McKinley stayed in this B&B while visiting the area. Fully re-decorated (includes air conditioned rooms), this charming B&B offers a hearty breakfast each morning. Four rooms include a lovely king size bedroom offering private entrance; an efficiency apartment with kitchen, private entrance and bath; and 2 additional rooms upstairs which share a living room, full kitchen and bath. No pets.

Daily $60-$80

Editor's Note: Reviewed in 1993. Warm hostess, comfortable accommodations and hearty breakfasts make this B&B appealing.

SURF-N-SAND   **(517) 856-4400**
                                               MOTEL/COTTAGES

Year around waterfront facility offers pool, A/C, and CATV. King and queen size beds available. Most major credit cards accepted.

Daily $68 (and up)

GRINDSTONE CITY

WHALEN'S GRINDSTONE SHORES   **(517) 738-7664**
                                                 CABINS

Located on the waterfront between mobile home/RV sites, this small but nicely wooded area features 11 units, in close proximity, with kitchen facilities. Handicap access. Major credit cards accepted.

Call for Rates

HURON CITY

LIGHTHOUSE RESORT   **(517) 428-4747**
                                             COTTAGES

Full kitchen facilities are featured in these cabins sitting on the waterfront of beautiful Lake Huron. Handicap access. Open year around.

Call for Rates

LEXINGTON

BEACHCOMBER MOTEL & APARTMENTS   **(810) 359-8859**
                                         COTTAGES/MOTEL

Offers motel units, efficiencies, family units, cottages with fireplaces. Sandy beach, swimming pool, boats, fishing, tennis court, A/C, color TV. Beach house bed and breakfast! Open all year.

Daily $45 (and up)

CENTENNIAL BED & BREAKFAST　　　　　　　　**(810) 359-8762**
DANIEL & DILLA MILLER　　　　　　　　　　**BED & BREAKFAST**

Elegant 1879 home listed on State Historic Register. Traditionally decorated with a touch of antiques. 4-poster beds and lace sets a warm and romantic mood. Smoke free environment. Gourmet breakfast. Close to beach and shops. Centennial is a piece of the romantic past.

Daily　　　　$55-$65

COZMA'S COTTAGES　　　　　**(810) 359-8150 • (810) 881-3313**
　　　　　　　　　　　　　　　　　　　　　　COTTAGES

The nicest feature of this lodging is the location which is set in a lovely park-like setting along 200 ft. of sandy beach. Volleyball/badminton court, BBQ grill, shuffleboard, horseshoes on grounds. These small cottages (sleep 4-6) offer clean but limited kitchens. Two newer mobile homes (sleeps 5-6) are also available for rent.

Weekly　　　$265 (and up)

LEX ON THE LAKE　　　　　　　　　　**(810) 359-7910**
　　　　　　　　　　　　　　　　　　　　　　COTTAGES

Situated on a narrow, wooded lot, these 8 older cabins offer kitchen facilities along with color CATV. Small but quiet and attractive sitting area which overlooks the water. Descending stairway takes you to the beach.

Daily　　　　$45 (and up)

LUSKY'S LAKEFRONT RESORT COTTAGES　　　　**(810) 327-6889**
　　　　　　　　　　　　　　　　　　　　　　COTTAGES

The friendly owners of Lusky's have completely refurbished (inside and out) all cottages in 1993! Clean, cozy and comfortable, each comes w/ceiling fans, cable TV, picnic tables, BBQ grills, fully equipped kitchens, private toilets (most w/private showers). Screened porches have good views of lake and play area. Play area features airplane swing, play boats, tire swirl, gymset w/ tube slide, large sandbox w/ crane and more. There's also volley ball, basketball, shuffleboard, paddleboats  and rowboats. Stop at our novelty store for candy, pop, ice cream and trinkets galore — at old fashioned prices! All this make for a fun, relaxing and affordable family vacation place where memories are made and treasured. Rentals available daily and weekly. Pets allowed.

Daily　　　$50 and up　　　Weekly　　　$275 and up

MICHIGAN COTTAGES • CHALETS • CONDOS • B&B'S

THE POWELL HOUSE   (810) 359-5533
NANCY POWELL   BED & BREAKFAST

This charming B&B is located on beautifully landscaped grounds.
Each of the four rooms offers their own separate charm and features
king and queen size beds. Two rooms w/private baths, two rooms
(suite) share a bath. Bicycles available for your leisurely tour of
historic Lexington. Full breakfast included.

Daily $65-$75 (depending on room)

BRITANNIA HOUSE   (810) 359-5772
HUGH & HANNAH LIDDIARO   BED & BREAKFAST

Grand 1874 brick Italianate home with ornate woodwork and arched windows.
On State and National Historic Registers. Guest rooms have marbled
fireplaces and featherbeds. Full English cooked breakfast daily. Evening
snacks. Easy walking distance to harbor, beach and quaint shops. Visa/MC.
No smoking. No pets. Let us treat you royally!

Daily $75 (dbl)

MARLEEN WILSON   (517) 635-3507
                                        VACATION HOME

Spacious 3,000 sq. ft. on 4 acres of wooded land with 250 ft. of beach front.
Stairway (42 steps) leads to the beach. The home features 4 bedrooms (sleeps
8), is completed furnished with fully equipped kitchen including stove,
refrigerator, coffee maker, washer, dryer, etc. Enjoy the scenic view of the
Blue Water Bridge at night. Only 20 minutes north of Port Huron. Security
deposit and payment required in advance.

Weekly $1,000

PORT AUSTIN

BLUE SPRUCE MOTEL   (517) 738-8651
                                        MOTEL/COTTAGES

Motel and cottages offer color CATV and AC. MC/Visa accepted.

Call for Rates

GARFIELD INN   (517) 738-5254
                                       BED & BREAKFAST

Visited by President Garfield in 1860, the inn not only features period antiques
but one of Michigan's premier restaurants! For that special occasion ask about
the "Presidential Room"! Rooms feature double and queen size beds.
Complementary bottle of champagne with each room and continental
breakfasts. Six rooms.

Daily $75-$95

52

Harbor Pines/North Shore Beach

(810) 650-9888
Condos

Two luxury condominiums, available year around, on 300 ft. of Lake Huron — tip of Michigan's thumb! Includes 2 bedrooms, 2 baths, sleep 6, fully furnished. Heat, air conditioning, CATV, VCR, and fireplaces. Playground area. Rental available weekly, monthly, or yearly. No pets.

Weekly $650 (Summer)

Krebs Beachside Cottages

(517) 856-2876
Cottages/Efficiencies

These 8 cottages (1-4 bedroom) sit on open, landscaped grounds with a scattering of large trees. Each lodging is fully furnished with living area (includes CATV), private baths, and equipped kitchens with microwave. Cribs available. Large wooden deck overlooks 200 ft. of sandy beach and offers a terrific view of the Saginaw Bay. Open May-October. Pets allowed in off-season.

Weekly $375 (and up) Reduced and daily rates available during spring/fall

Editor's Note: Reviewed in 1993. Unpretentious, clean, comfortable lodgings on spacious grounds, affordably priced with warm and caring owners make this a choice spot to stay — reserve early.

Kreb's Lane Cottages

(313) 886-5752 • (517) 738-8548
Cottages/Efficiencies

Set vertically to the water, these 8 clean, well maintained 2 bedroom cottages and efficiencies sit on a small lot with 50 ft. of sandy beach on Saginaw Bay. Includes equipped kitchens (some with microwaves), CATV and cribs. Some cottages/efficiencies offer knotty pine interiors and lake views. Open May-September. Call for special holiday packages. No pets.

Weekly $450

Lake Vista Motel & Cottage Resort

Mary Gottschalk

(517) 738-8612
Motel/Cottages

On the shores of Lake Huron and Saginaw Bay. Motel units with queen size beds, color cable and air conditioning. Efficiency cottages with two double beds and queen size sofa sleeper. Refrigerator, stove, microwave, showers, dishes, and toaster. Recreational area, heated pool, snack bar. Bait and tackle. No pets. Call for brochure.

Weekly $440 (and up)

MICHIGAN COTTAGES • CHALETS • CONDOS • B&B'S

LAKE STREET MANOR   **(517) 738-7720**
                                                            BED & BREAKFAST

This 5 room B&B, built in 1875 by a lumber baron, is furnished with antiques and features large bays, high peaked roof and gingerbread trim. Comfortably furnished with hot tub and in-room movies. Both private and shared baths offered. Brick BBQ's and bikes offered for guests' enjoyment. Fenced 1/2 acre.

Daily $50-$60

OSENTOSKI REALTY/LAKEFRONT CONDO'S   **(517) 738-5251**
                                                            CONDOS

Spacious condos located on the beautiful shores of Lake Huron. 1 and 2 bedroom units feature fireplaces, CATV fully equipped kitchens and much, much more. Open all year.

Weekly $500 (and up)

THE CASTAWAYS BEACH RESORT & MOTOR INN   **(517) 738-5101**
                                                            MOTEL/COTTAGES

Located along 400' of Lake Huron shoreline, this resort offers 46 rooms, dining room and lounge. Also swimming pool, AC, Color CATV, and handicap accessibility. MC/Visa accepted. Open all year. AAA rated.

Call for Rates

TOWN CENTER COTTAGES   **(800) 848-4184 • (517) 738-7223**
                                                            COTTAGES

In the heart of it all! Two bedroom cottages with full kitchens, CATV, screened front porch and a very private outdoor area for family fun. Visa/MC/personal checks gladly accepted.

Daily $55   Weekly $300
  (Off-season and AARP Discounts available)

WINDY HILL LODGE   **(517) 738-8650**
                                                            LODGE

This lodge offers 10 rooms with five 2 room suites that share a bath. Queen size beds available. Access to tennis courts and health club. Personal checks, MC/Visa accepted. Great for family groups.

Call for Rates

PORT HOPE

STAFFORD HOUSE   **(517) 428-4554**
PATRICIA BARAN   BED & BREAKFAST
Only one block from Lake Huron, this nicely maintained B&B sits on an attractive open treed lot with a lovely backyard wildflower garden. Open year around,. Full breakfasts served each morning. 4 rooms (one suite overlooks garden and is air conditioned).

Daily $45-$75

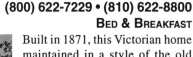

PORT SANILAC

RAYMOND HOUSE INN   **(800) 622-7229 • (810) 622-8800**
BED & BREAKFAST

Built in 1871, this Victorian home maintained in a style of the old port village, offers 7 large high-ceiling bedrooms (all w/private baths) and central A/C. Each room is finished with period furniture and brightly colored bedspreads and lace curtains. An old-fashioned parlor and dining room, unchanged in a century, adds to the warmth and charm of this lodging. Open mid-April through December. Antique shop/art gallery on premises. No smoking. No pets.

Daily $55-$70

SEBEWAING

RUMMELS TREE HAVEN B&B   **(517) 883-2450**
CARL & ERMA RUMMEL, JR.   **BED & BREAKFAST**

A 2 room bed & breakfast with full breakfast that features private bath, cable TV, AC, refrigerator, microwave. Fishing for perch and walleye. If you are a hunter—then this area is good for duck, goose, deer, and pheasant. Personal checks accepted. Open all year. Pets allowed in garage area.

Daily $31 (and up —price includes tax)

UNIONVILLE

FISH POINT LODGE   **(517) 674-2631**
LODGE

Located near Fish Point game reserve this lodge, built in 1902, offers 4 bedrooms, shared bath and a huge fireplace. Kitchen facilities are available. 15-20 people can be accommodated at one time. Breakfast is included. Personal check OK. Open year around.

Call for Rates

BAY CITY • FRANKENMUTH • SAGINAW

Bay City, well known for its water sports, features a variety of events including speedboat and offshore power boat races. Tour the city's many historical sites and view the many stately homes on Center Avenue, Wenonah and Veterans Memorial parks. Come south from Bay City and explore the historic district of **Saginaw**. Take a four-mile river walk, visit a museum or the zoo and stroll among the fragrant rose gardens in downtown parks.

Traveling south from Saginaw, you'll reach the historic town of **Frankenmuth.** The classic Bavarian stylings of its original settlers can be seen throughout the town's homes, buildings and craft shops. For many, over the generations, it has become a traditional yearly visit. They come to the more than 100 shops and attractions, stroll the streets, tour the wineries and brewery, sample traditional German cuisine or their famous *all you can eat* chicken dinners. While there are many good places to eat in the area, The *Bavarian Inn* and *Zehnder's* are still the most popular...and *beware* their bakeries are *too* tempting!!

While you're in Frankenmuth, be sure to take a horse-drawn carriage or a river tour. And, of course, you must visit Bronner's Christmas Wonderland where holidays are celebrated 363 days a year. Spend the night, because you'll want to get started shopping early the next morning at the areas largest designer outlet shopping mall located only a few minutes away in Birch Run!!

For additional information on special events in these areas, contact:

Frankenmuth CVB
635 South Main Street
Frankenmuth, MI 48734
(517) 652-6106

Bay County CVB
315 14th St.
Bay City, MI 48708
(517) 892-1222

Saginaw CVB
901 S. Washington Ave.
Saginaw, MI 48601
(800) 444-9979 • (517) 752-7164

BAY CITY

CLEMENTS INN   **(517) 894-4600**
KAREN HEPP   **BED & BREAKFAST**
Under new ownership in 1994, this 1886 Victorian mansion offers 6 elaborately furnished guest rooms w/private baths and phones, 6 fireplaces, central A/C. Enjoy the newly decorated 500 sq. ft. whirlpool suite or the spacious 1,600 sq. ft. "family" suite which features bedroom, full kitchen, bath, living and dining room.

Daily $70-$125

STONEHEDGE INN   **(517) 894-4342**
RUTH KOERBER   **BED & BREAKFAST**
Built by a lumber baron, this 1889 English Tudor home is indeed an elegant journey into the past. Original fireplaces, stained glass windows, speaking tubes and warming oven. Magnificent open foyer with its grand oak staircase leads to eight bedrooms. Ideal for small weddings, parties, meetings. Corporate rates Sunday-Thursday

Daily $75-$85

FRANKENMUTH

BED AND BREAKFAST AT THE PINES   **(517) 652-9019**
RICHARD & DONNA HODGE   **BED & BREAKFAST**
Welcome to our casual ranch-style home in a quiet residential neighborhood, within walking distance of famous restaurants and main tourist areas. Double and twin beds. Wholesome nutritious breakfast featuring homemade baked items, fresh fruit, jams and beverages. Open year around. 2 rooms.. No smoking.

Daily $30-$45

BENDER HAUS BED AND BREAKFAST   **(517) 652-8897**
ELDEN & BEVERLEY BENDER   **BED & BREAKFAST**
Located in the center of town in a quiet residential area. Each uniquely decorated room offers either queen, double or twin beds with private or shared baths. A/C, TVs. Host is a direct descendant of the first immigrants of Frankenmuth. 4 rooms.. No smoking. German and English spoken.

Daily $55-$65

SAGINAW

BROCKWAY HOUSE BED & BREAKFAST   **(800) 383-5043 • (517) 792-0746**
THE ZUEHLKES   **BED & BREAKFAST**
On the National Register of Historic Sites, this 1864 B&B is built in the
grand tradition of the old southern plantation. Near to excellent restaurants
and antique shops. 4 rooms with private baths. Jucuzzi suite available.

Daily $85-$175

HEART HOUSE INN   **(517) 753-3145**
KELLY & KURT ZURVALEC   **BED & BREAKFAST**
This 8,000 sq. ft. mansion, built during the Civil War, features black walnut
beams and lumber throughout. All 8 rooms with private bath, phones, TV, A/
C, complimentary local daily paper. "Continental Plus Breakfast". Public din-
ing during lunch/dinner hours. Liquor License. Major credit cards accepted.

Daily $45-$75

REGION 2

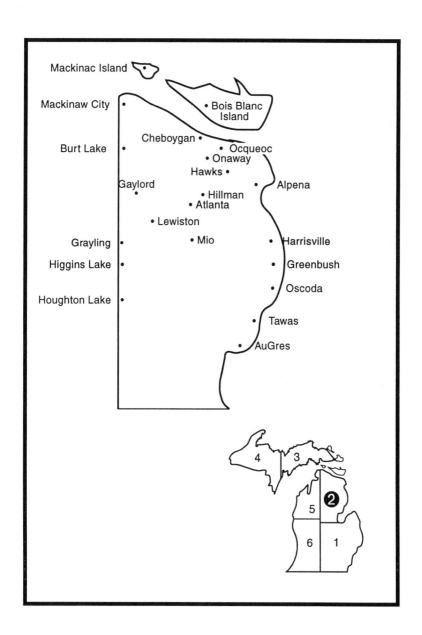

REGION 2

Progressing northward, the forest grows denser, filled with sparkling lakes and streams. Here is canoeing, skiing and abundant fishing, fine places to eat, festivals, art fairs and scenic beauty as far as the eye can see.

Going east, to Lake Huron, we enter the land where lumber once was *King*, the land of the *River Rat* and the *Legend of Paul Bunyan*. More money was made here on lumber than miners made in the Klondike during the Gold Rush. Stripped bare by lumbering frenzy, in 1909 the reforestation began. Today the forests are tall and stately and the forest floors are deep again with pine needles and teaming with wild life. Throughout the forest there are lakes, trout streams and fishing at its best. In the winter, when the forests floor is covered by snow, you will see not only the markings of elk, deer and moose, but also those of snowshoe, snowmobile and ski trails.

The days along the Huron are filled with activities throughout the seasons — sandy beaches, good swimming, tournaments, museums, lighthouses, historic sights, but most of all the scenic beauty and wonders of nature. The morning is a gentle symphony as the sun rises, a golden globe, out of the Huron and the breezes whisper through the pines mingling with the sound of the birds.

Yes, here is the excitement, beauty, peace and tranquillity!

OSCODA & THE AUSABLE AREA

Covers: AuGres • East Tawas • Greenbush • Harrisville • Mio

Experience the open hospitality of **AuGres** as you continue to travel north on Michigan's east side. The restaurants and bake shops here are truly homey with freshly prepared meals. Considered the "Perch Capital", this small town has more than 1,000 boat docks and waters well stocked with perch, walleye and a large variety of pan fish. The best scenic views can be found along the lake shore roads, from Point AuGres and Point Lookout. Take your boat to Charity Island and explore its "most photographed" lighthouse. Excellent golf is available at Huron Breeze Golf & Country Club or, for the whole family, visit Lutz's Fun Land featuring waterslides, go-carts, and a variety of games and rides.

Settled where the AuSable River meets Lake Huron, these series of communities offer a variety of activities from canoeing and fishing to hiking, hunting, cross-country skiing, and snowmobiling. **Oscoda** is considered the gateway to the River Road National Scenic Byway that runs along the south bank of the AuSable River. **Tawas City** and nearby Huron National Forest offers lakes, beaches and great trails! During winter season, cross-country ski enthusiasts can enjoy the well-groomed trails at Corseair. In February, the Perchville U.S.A. Festival takes place — be there to enjoy the festivities!

The quaint harbor town of **Harrisville** offers terrific trout and salmon fishing. The Sturgeon Point Lighthouse Museum, a summer concert series, art and craft fairs, festivals, and the Harrisville State Park provide a variety of both summer and winter recreational fun.

Mio, the Heart of the AuSable River Valley, excels in canoeing and winter sport activities. In June they host the Championship Canoe Race and the Great Lakes Forestry Exposition in July. While there, tour the Kirtland warbler nesting area.

To sample some of the area's down home cooking, try *The Bear Track Inn* (AuGres) noted for outstanding breakfast buffets plus a diverse menu including, of course, excellent fish! *H&H Bakery* (AuGres) features excellent fresh baked goods daily...their specialty is pizza! *Charbonneau* (on the AuSable in Oscoda) for a diverse menu on the waterfront; *Wiltse's* (Oscoda) for some of the best blueberry pancakes around; and *Muehlbeck's* (Harrisville) for some freshly prepared German food. Also, we've heard the *Greenbush Tavern* offers up some pretty good pizza and "all you can eat" fish on Friday. If you happen to be in Tawas, stop by the *Tawas Bar* and tell them Bonnie sent you.

OSCODA & THE AUSABLE AREA

*(Continued...)_*

For additional information on special events in the Oscoda & AuSable area, contact:

Oscoda-AuSable Chamber of Com.
100 W. Michigan Avenue
Oscoda, MI 48750
(800) 235-GOAL (MI only)
 -or- (517) 739-7322

Huron Shores Chamber of Com.
P.O. Box 151
Harrisvillle, MI 48740
(517) 724-5107

Mio Area Chamber of Commerce
210 S. Morenci, Mio, MI 48647
(517) 826-3331

AUGRES

THE GET-A-WAY
TOM & KAREN WILSON

(313) 389-1793
PRIVATE COTTAGE

Year-round waterfront cottage on a 70' landscaped lot on the tip of Pt. AuGres. Beautiful vistas of Lake Huron/Saginaw Bay. 3 bedrooms, 1 bath, sleeps 6, linens provided, fully equipped kitchen with modern appliances. Patio, charcoal grill, play area, TV/VCR. Security deposit required. **No Pets.** Marina 1 mile, restaurant/bar walking distance. Call for additional information.

Rates $450 (plus $150 security deposit)

EAST TAWAS

EAST TAWAS JUNCTION B&B

(517) 362-8006
BED & BREAKFAST

This Victorian style B&B overlooks Tawas Bay and sits upon an estate sized, treed lot. The 4 guest rooms offer private baths, separate guest entrance. Enjoy the comfort of the large parlor w/fireplace, enclosed porch, sun deck, CATV and more! Full breakfasts. 4 rooms. Close to harbor, sandy beaches and shops.

Daily $40-$80

RIPTIDE MOTEL & CABINS **(517) 362-6562**
EMMA & LARRY, MANAGERS **MOTEL & CABINS**

On Tawas Bay, this year around resort features large sandy beach, picnic tables, play area, CATV and BBQ grills. In addition to their motel rooms, Riptide offers 4, 2 bedroom cabins with equipped kitchens and private baths (linens provided). No pets in summer.

Daily $38-$76   Weekly $370 (cabins, assumes 5 days)

GREENBUSH

SID'S RESORT **(517) 739-7638 • (810) 781-3845**
COTTAGES

These 11, 1-3 bedroom cottages (sleep 2-8) had major renovations in 1993-94 including new interiors (custom draperies, dishes, etc.). Set on wooded grounds with excellent sandy swimming beach, these fully furnished lodgings offer equipped kitchen, CATV, and more. Game room, shuffleboard, badminton, playground and picnic area on premises. Water bicycles, paddle boards, kayak and wave runners available. Near many golf courses. Open May - Oct. No pets.

Weekly $385-$1,000 (Reduced off-season rates in spring and fall)

HARRISVILLE

BIG PAW RESORT **(517) 724-6326**
COTTAGES/EFFICIENCIES

On the shores of Lake Huron. This premiere resort has fully furnished, well maintained lodgings offering secluded comfort. Lovely views, fireplaces, CATV, radios, refrigerators, coffee makers. Three cottages accommodate 2 to 7 people (1 to 3 bedrooms) and are separated by 100 feet of gardens and woodlands. Remaining units are in motel-like arrangement. Rates include breakfast and dinner. Open May-Oct.

Daily $90-$105*   Weekly $630-$735*

* Per adult. Children rates somewhat less. Reduced off-season & package rates available.

Editor's Note: Reviewed in 1993. Very comfortable, clean, terrific setting with freshly prepared, delicious meals served daily. A bit pricey but well worth it. This one is a favorite with many of our readers too!

MICHIGAN COTTAGES • CHALETS • CONDOS • B&B'S

CEDAR CREST
MR. & MRS. CALLAS

(313) 871-8500 • (313) 881-7611
COTTAGE

Private cottage on Cedar Lake sits on 6 wooded acres. Includes use of canoe and rowboat. Private golf and beach club (2 courses) including Scottish Links. Cottage has 2 bedrooms, 1-1/2 baths, kitchen, den and living room with fireplace. Sleeps 8. Large screened front porch and rear deck overlooking Lake.

Weekly $400

MIO

HINCHMAN ACRE RESORT

(800) 438-0203 • (517) 826-3267
COTTAGES

Borders the AuSable River. Open all year. Canoe rentals/trips, game room, shuffleboard, horseshoes, trout fishing, hiking trails and more. Great hunting, x-country ski in winter. 1 to 3 bedroom cottages furnished w/fully equipped kitchens (includes linens and towels). Bathrooms with stall showers or tub-stall. CATV. Several cottages with fireplaces, A/C, and electric heat.

Daily $35-$85   Weekly $230-$450

OSCODA

ANCHORAGE COTTAGES
PEG GRICE

(517) 739-7843
COTTAGES

Unpack & RELAX! On our sugar sand beach, Lake Huron. Six clean, comfortable, fully furnished cottages (1-4 bedrooms). CATV, grills, picnic tables, shady backyard, fire pit, horseshoes, swing set. AuSable River nearby. Fish, golf, canoe, hunt, etc. Friendly atmosphere! Pet w/approval/Fee. April-Dec.

Call for Brochure and Rates

AUSABLE RIVER RESORT

(517) 739-5246
COTTAGES

Two bedroom cottages w/kitchen and color TV, only 1/2 mile west of downtown Oscoda on the waterfront. Boat dockage available.

Call for Rates

BAREFOOT BEACH COTTAGES
THE STRATTONS
(517) 739-1818
COTTAGES

Seven furnished cottages (sleep 4-6) w/private showers on 200 ft. of sandy beach along Lake Huron. Swimming is safe and fun. Resort features swings, loungers, rowboats, paddleboats, grills, bonfire pit & more. Linens supplied. Bring towels. $50 deposit. No pets.

Call for Rates

EAST COAST SHORES RESORT
TOM TREVILLIAN
(517) 739-0123
CABINS

On 200 ft. of sandy beach, fully furnished cabins have equipped kitchens (includes microwave, automatic coffee pot, picnic table and grill). Beachfront cabins include 1-2 bedrooms w/screened porch, beach chairs. Enjoy volleyball, badminton, horseshoes, bonfires and swimming.

Call for Rates

EL CORTEZ BEACH RESORT
(517) 739-7884
COTTAGES

On Lake Huron these 1-2 bedroom cottages offer equipped kitchens, gas heat, city water, CATV w/HBO. Linens provided. Enjoy the family fun area, BBQ's, picnic tables, and large sandy beach. Charter a fishing boat with USCA licensed crew. Fish cleaning station on premises. No pets.

Call for Rates

HURON HOUSE
(517) 739-9255
BED & BREAKFAST

On Lake Huron, between Tawas and Oscoda, enjoy the excellent sunrises and romantic moonlit beaches. 8 guest rooms include A/C and private baths. Relax in the hot tub or on one of the three large decks overlooking the water. Convenient to many area activities.

Daily $55-$85 dbl.

NEW AUSABLE BEACH RESORT
RON TEASLEY
(517) 739-9971
COTTAGES

Located 2 miles south of Oscoda on Lake Huron, these 1-3 bedroom cottages offer fully equipped kitchens, showers, carpeting. Some cottages w/fireplaces. Enjoy horseshoes, playground and sandy beach.

Call for Rates

OSCODA RESORT
(517) 739-2714
CONDOMINIUM/DUPLEXES

These lodgings offer 10 clean housekeeping units located north of Oscoda on Lake Huron. Each unit features CATV (w/HBO), gas log fireplaces. Large wooden sun deck overlooks the lake.

Call for Rates

MICHIGAN COTTAGES • CHALETS • CONDOS • B&B'S

SAND CASTLE   **(517) 739-9881**
M/M INGLINS   COTTAGES

Five, 1-2 bedroom cottages located on the beach. Includes fully equipped kitchen (linens provided), CATV, shuffleboard, volleyball, fish cleaning area and more.

Weekly $240 (and up)

SHADY SHORES RESORT   **(810) 852-1103 • (313) 526-9885**
KENT & JEANNE LANG/JIM & MARYANN GROSS   COTTAGES

Three miles south of Oscoda, this resort offers 200' of sandy beach, picnic tables, BBQ's, swings, horseshoe pits, basketball and shuffleboard courts. Each 2 bedroom cottage (w/double bed) is furnished and has CATV. Kitchens include refrigerator, range and dishes. Linens provided (bring your own towels). Most have glassed-in porch. No pets.

Call for Rates

SHENANDOAH ON THE LAKE BEACH RESORT   **(517) 739-3997**
                                       COTTAGES

The resort, 2 miles south of Oscoda on Lake Huron w/400' sandy beach, has 1 and 2 bedroom cottages + 6 spacious 3 bedroom beachhouses. Each has fully equipped kitchen (some w/fireplaces), decks, CATV, recreation area, campfires. Open year around. Pets allowed (off-season).

Call for Rates

THOMAS' PARKSIDE COTTAGES   **(517) 739-5607**
                                       COTTAGES

On Lake Huron w/300 ft. of private beach, the cottages are near the AuSable River. Includes 2, 1 bedroom and 11, 2 bedroom cottages facing the lake with enclosed porches, kitchen w/stove and refrigerator, CATV. Bring radio and linens. $50 deposit. No pets.

Call for Rates

ALPENA & THUNDER BAY

COVERS: ALPENA • ATLANTA • HAWKS • HILLMAN • OCQUEOC • ONAWAY

Located on the beautiful sunrise side of Michigan, visitors can enjoy a variety of activities — summer through winter. Explore **Thunder Bay's** underwater ruins of sunken ships from another era. Or, for something a little less exerting, enjoy **Alpena's** "live" theater which presents year around plays and musicals. The area also offers a wildfowl sanctuary, lighthouses, and excellent hunting, fishing, cross-country skiing, and golf. Don't miss July's Brown Trout Festival which lures (excuse the pun...) over 800 fishing contestants to this nine-day event featuring art, food concessions and nightly entertainment.

While in the area, don't forget to visit one of the Lower Peninsula's largest waterfalls, Ocqueoc Falls, in Rogers City.

Convention/Visitor's Bureau of Thunder Bay Region
P.O. Box 65, Alpena, MI 49707
(800) 582-1906 -or- (517) 354-4181

ALPENA

COMERFORD'S BIRCH SHORES RESORT
(517) 595-6208
CABINS

Lovely park-like setting overlooking a quiet stretch of Grand Lake. These 1-2 bedroom cottages offer fireplaces. Provide your own linens. Included in rental price is 14 ft. aluminum boat. Outboard motors, pontoon, paddleboat, canoe rentals available. Closed March and April.

Daily $40 (and up)   Weekly $200 (and up)

Editor's Note: Visited in 1993. Excellent location on Grand Lake. Resort offers nice features but some cabins needed updating.

FIRESIDE INN
(517) 595-6369
COTTAGES & LODGE

Set in densely wooded surroundings, this resort built in 1908, offers 17 cottage/cabins and 7 lodge rooms. Some cottages are newly renovated while others maintain a "rustic" image. All have private baths. Some with kitchen and fireplaces. Lodge offers small sleeping rooms, some with private baths. Tennis, volleyball, ping-pong, horseshoes, shuffleboard on premises. Price includes 2 meals per day. Open Spring through Fall. Pets allowed.

	Rooms	Cabins/Cottages
Daily*	$27-$32	$37-$70
Weekly*	$150-$185	$210-$300

* Price based per adult (children rates somewhat less)

MICHIGAN COTTAGES • CHALETS • CONDOS • B&B'S

JOE HASSETT   (517) 734-2066 (AFTER 4 P.M.)
                                     COTTAGE

One cottage located on US 23 South. It is south of Bluebird Restaurant (2 bedrooms) on Grand Lake.

Weekly $250

TRELAWNY RESORT   (517) 471-2347
                                       COTTAGES

On Lake Huron's Thunder Bay w/200 feet of sandy beach these eight small to moderate sized, 1-2 bedroom cottages are fully furnished with equipped kitchens and shower/bath. Blankets and pillows provided. Excellent swimming/ fishing. Near Timber Creek Ski Lodge. Playground, volleyball, shuffleboard, horseshoes. No pets.

Daily $45-$65 (and up)

ATLANTA

RIVER CABINS   (517) 785-4123
                                       CABINS

One mile west of Atlanta on M32, 1/2 Mile south on McArthur and Thunder Bay River, these 5, 1-2 bedroom cabins offer furnace heat, cooking facilities, linens, plus a boat with each cabin. Bathhouse w/shower, picnic tables, fire ring on premises.

Daily $25-$35

HAWKS

NETTIE BAY LODGE   (517) 734-4688
MARK & JACKIE SCHULER   LODGE

Year around resort on 2,000 acres of secluded private property on Bullhead Lake. One to 4 bedrooms with full kitchens, living room, private baths (linens available), and lake views. Into bird watching? Nettie Bay is where you want to go! Mentioned in *Michigan-Out-of Doors* magazine and other media. Join them in classes, seminars and their birding walks. Also enjoy excellent fishing and x-country skiing. No pets.

Weekly $275-$440

HILLMAN

THUNDER BAY RESORT
(800) 729-9375
CONDOMINIUM/VILLAS

The resort offers luxury condominium and villa accommodations for golf, bow hunting, cross country ski and snowmobile enthusiasts. Contemporary in design, each lodging is fully furnished and include kitchens/kitchenettes. Special week/weekend packages available. Dining on premises.

Daily $41-$56 and up*

*Per person/quad occupancy. Ask about special weekend/week packages for golf/x-country skiing.

OCQUEOC

ANDERSON'S PI-NO-LA RESORT
(517) 733-8969
COTTAGES

Two housekeeping cottages on Ocqueoc Lake are located between Onaway, Rogers City and Cheboygan. Parking for boats available. No more than 5 hp. motor allowed (no water skiing). 240 acres of private hunting land. Boat included w/rental. Open Memorial Day weekend-Nov.

Call for Rates

SILVER ROCK RESORT ON OCQUEOC LAKE
(810) 694-3061
STEVE & VICKI KELLAR   COTTAGE

Ocqueoc Lake is a 132 acre lake twenty miles north of Rogers City and three miles west of Lake Huron. Two bedroom cottage with boat, color TV. ORV trails nearby. Great fishing for bass, walleye, pike, trout and salmon. Open all year. Call for rates and reservations. No pets.

Call for Rates

MANTOURE'S CABINS
(517) 734-2421
CABINS

Located approx. 15 mile north of Rogers City, 4 cabins are offered and include TV, private showers, ranges, refrigerators, dishes and pans. Boat and trailer parking available. No housekeeping. Open May-Nov.

Call for Rates

ONAWAY

STILLMEADOW B & B
CAROL LATSCH

(517) 733-2882
BED & BREAKFAST

Flower beds, kitchen garden and berry patch add to the charm of this simple country home, nestled at woods edge, with large deck for relaxing and enjoying the view. Four rooms, private baths, queen beds and a tasty country breakfast to start your day. Radios, CATV and stereo in public room. Smoke-free environment. Pets allowed leashed outside. Visa & Mastercard.

Daily $60-$80

Editor's Note: This charming B&B offers a comfortable and relaxing country atmosphere with freshly prepared, hearty breakfasts! Carol is truly knowledgeable about the area — things to do and see. See our review this edition!

MACKINAW CITY • MACKINAC ISLAND

Near the tip of the mitt, **Mackinaw City** is located at the southern end of the Mackinac Bridge and offers ferry service (May-October) to Mackinac Island. Known for its sparkling waters and natural beauty, it is visited by thousands of vacationers each year. While in the City, be sure to visit Fort Michilimackinaw. Built in 1715, the Fort was initially used as a trading post by early French settlers before becoming a British military outpost and fur-trading village. Today its costumed staff provide demonstrations and special programs. Mackinaw City also offers a variety of other historical parks (several with archaeological excavations in progress), unique museums and souvenir shops.

Visit **Mackinac Island** and step back in time. This unhurried vacation land is a haven for any vacationer wishing a unique experience. Accessible by ferry, the Island allows only horse-drawn carriages and bicycles to be used as transportation. Historical and scenic, the Island is filled with natural beauty and boasts a colorful past. Explore Old Fort Mackinac where costumed staff perform period military reenactments and demonstrations. Take a carriage tour, visit nearby historic buildings and homes and browse the many shops. Enjoy nightly entertainment, golfing, swimming, hiking, horseback riding, and just relaxing on this Michigan resort island. There are also many great restaurants on the island! For an elegant, fine dining experience, there's the 107 year old

MACKINAW CITY • MACKINAC ISLAND

(continued...)

Grand Hotel's formal dining room. Or, on the northwest side of the island, *Woods* is the spot for a romantic, candlelight dinner located in Stonecliffe, a mansion built in 1905. For more casual dining with exceptional food, try the *Point Dining Room* at the Mission Point Resort. Hangout with the locals, and try the down-to-earth *Mustang Lounge* (one of the few places open year around). Enjoy your trip to the island ...oh, by the way, don't forget to bring home the fudge!

For additional information regarding events and activities in the area contact:

Greater Mackinaw City Chamber of Com.
706 S. Huron Street
Mackinaw City, MI 49701
(616) 436-5574

Mackinac Island Chamber of Com.
P.O. Box 451,
Mackinac Island, MI 49757
(906) 847-3783

MACKINAW CITY

THE BEACH HOUSE

(800) 262-5353 • (616) 436-5353
COTTAGES

Situated on 250' of Lake Huron frontage, view the Bridge and Island from these 1-3 bed cottages in Mackinaw City. Units include kitchenettes (no utensils), electric heat, A/C, CATV w/HBO. Coffee and homemade muffins available each morning! Playground, beach, indoor pool and spa on the premises. Small pets allowed.

Daily $32-$110

Editor's Note: Good, clean, comfortable accommodations!

CEDARS RESORT

(616) 537-4748
COTTAGES

On Lake Huron, 5 miles from Mackinaw, these 1-2 bedroom cottages offer a great view of the Bridge and Island! Each unit offers full housekeeping and includes equipped kitchens, bathroom, fireplace (wood furnished), gas heat, and color TV. Sandy beach great for swimming - boat and docking included. Open year around. $75 deposit required.

Weekly $290

71

MICHIGAN COTTAGES • CHALETS • CONDOS • B&B'S

CHIPPEWA MOTOR LODGE - ON THE LAKE   **(800) 748-0124 • (616) 436-8661**
MOTEL/COTTAGES

In addition to its motel accommodations, the lodge offers 2 bedroom cottage units (double/queen size beds). The lodge is located on sandy beach and features CATV, direct dial phones, indoor pool and spa, sun deck, shuffleboard, picnic area. Only 1 block from ferry docks.

Daily $27-$88*   Weekly $200-$525*
*Based on double occupancy. Rates will vary depending on season.

Editor's Note: Clean and very nicely maintained. Many rooms have cozy, paneled interiors.

LAKESHORE PARADISE   **(616) 537-4779**
COTTAGES

Approximately 5 miles south of Mackinaw with 250' lake frontage, 1-2 bedroom housekeeping cottages with heat, stoves and refrigerators. Some tubs and TVs. Playground, picnic tables, grills on premises, raft in water, bonfires on beach. Open May 15 to Sept. 15.

Call for Rates

MACKINAC ISLAND

BAY VIEW AT MACKINAC   **(906) 847-3295 OR WINTER (615) 298-2759**
DOUG YODER   **BED & BREAKFAST**
This Victorian home offers grace and charm in romantic turn-of-the century tradition along with the comfort of today. It is the only facility of its type and style sitting at the water's edge. Deluxe continental breakfast served from harbor-view veranda. Private baths. Open May 1-Oct. 15. 17 rooms.

Daily $95-$185

CLOGHAUN   **(906) 847-3885 • WINTER (313) 331-7110**
DOROTHY & JAMES BOND   **BED & BREAKFAST**
This large Victorian home is convenient to shops, restaurants and ferry lines. Built in 1884, it was the home of Thomas and Bridgett Donnelly's large Irish family. Today, guests enjoy the many fine antiques, ambiance and elegance of a bygone era. Open May-Sept. 10 rooms.

Daily $60-$105

GREAT TURTLE LODGE   **(906) 847-6237**
NORM BAUMAN   **CONDOS/APARTMENTS**
Newly renovated in 1994, these two condo/apartments offer fully equipped kitchens, Jacuzzi's (TVs and VCR available). One bedroom sleeps 4-5, two bedroom sleeps 7-8. Located in a quiet wooded area of the Island — close to town. Minimum 2-3 night stay.

	1 Bedroom	2 Bedroom
Daily	$180	$200
Weekly	$1,000	$1,200

HAAN'S 1830 INN   **SUMMER (906) 847-6244 • WINTER (708) 526-2662**
NICHOLAS & NANCY HAAN   **BED & BREAKFAST**
This Michigan historic home, built in Greek Revival style, is furnished in period antiques. The earliest building was used as an inn in both Michigan and Wisconsin. Enjoy continental breakfast on the wicker filled porch. Featured in Detroit Free Press, Chicago Tribune, Chicago Sun Times and Sears Discovery Magazine. Open May 21-Oct. 18. 7 rooms. 5 with private bath and 2 w/shared bath.

Daily $80-$120

ISLAND CONDO RENTALS   **(906) 847-3260**
       CONDOMINIUMS
15 vacation rentals available on the Island. Call for information on daily and weekly rates.

METIVIER INN   **(906) 847-6234 • WINTER (616) 627-2055**
MICHAEL & JANICE GRAVES   **BED & BREAKFAST**
Originally built in 1877 and recently renovated, the Inn offers bedrooms with queen size beds and private baths. An efficiency unit is also available. Relax on the large wicker filled front porch and cozy living room with a wood burner. Deluxe continental breakfast served. Open May-October. 21 rooms.

Daily $88-$165

HOUGHTON LAKE TO CHEBOYGAN & BOIS BLANC ISLAND

COVERS: BURT LAKE • GAYLORD • GRAYLING • HIGGINS LAKE • LEWISTON • MULLETT LAKE

Houghton Lake, where hunters and vacationers thrive on one of Michigan's largest inland lakes. Enjoy hunting, boating, water skiing, cross-country skiing, and snowmobiling. Ice fishing for walleyes, bass and bluegill is so good it merits its own annual event. Each year, the Tip-Up-Town U.S.A. Festival (held mid to late January) offers a variety of events including contests, parades and games for the entire family.

Known as the "Alpine *Village*", **Gaylord** has more to offer than just great downhill and x-country skiing or groomed snowmobile trails! Try their championship golf courses or terrific year around fishing. Nearby, the largest elk herd roams, east of the Mississippi, in the Pigeon River State Forest.

Grayling, considered the "Canoe Capital of Michigan" is a most popular spot for canoeing and trout fishing! Its historical logging background is preserved at Crawford County Historical Museum and Hartwick Pines State Park.

Cheboygan continues the chain of great year around fishing, skiing, snowmobiling, swimming and golf. Be sure to visit Cheboygan's Opera House built in 1877. This restored Victorian theater still offers great entertainment on the same stage that once welcomed Mary Pickford and Annie Oakley!

Seeking an island retreat — without all the bustling activities on Mackinac Island — **Bois Blanc Island** is your spot! Referred to as *Bob-lo* by the locals, this quiet, unspoiled island is only a short boat ride from Cheboygan and Mackinac Island. One main road (unpaved) takes you around the Island (cars are permitted). An excellent spot for nature hikes, private beaches, boating and relaxing. Here is a community of century homes and a remote lighthouse. While visiting, stop in for "eats" at the *Boathouse Restaurant* or the *Bois Blanc Tavern* and meet some of the warm and friendly year around residents!

The Island is accessible by two ferry boat services (runs several times per day). Be sure to call ahead and reserve a spot if you plan on bringing your car (Plaunt Transportation: (616) 627-2354 or The Island Ferry Service (616) 627-9445 or (616) 627-7878).

HOUGHTON LAKE TO CHEBOYGAN & BOIS BLANC ISLAND

(continued...)

For additional information on events and activities in these areas contact:

Houghton Lake Chamber of Com.
1625 W. Houghton Lake Drive
Houghton Lake MI 48629
(800) 248-LAKE

Gaylord Area CVB
125 S. Otsego Avenue
Gaylord, MI 49735
(800) 342-9567

Grayling Chamber of Com.
P.O. Box 406
Grayling, MI 49738
(517) 348-2921

Cheboygan Chamber of Com.
P.O. Box 69
Cheboygan, MI 49721
(616) 627-7183

BOIS BLANC ISLAND

Bois Blanc Island Retreat **(616) 634-7435**
Gram/Linda McGeorge COTTAGE

Secluded, 4 bedroom, waterfront cottage on quiet protected bay. Surrounded by white pines and cedar forest. Beautiful view of Lake Huron and the Straits Channel. Cottage offers all the conveniences in a private setting — just bring groceries and fishing pole. Relax, fish, hike, explore, boat mooring. Mackinac Island 8 Miles. Open June-Nov. Car ferry. No pets.

Weekly $450-$650

Editor's Note: Comfortable, clean, newer cottage which should have all renovations completed by 1995. Great island retreat! See our review in this edition!

BURT LAKE

DiPietro Cottage **(517) 626-6682**
Robbe DiPietro COTTAGE
Private, wooded frontage on Burt Lake in the beautiful Maple Bay area. Cozy cottage with 4 bedrooms, complete modern kitchen, washer, dryer, dishwasher,

MICHIGAN COTTAGES • CHALETS • CONDOS • B&B'S

DIPIETRO COTTAGE (continued...)

wood stove, dock and boat hoist. Provide your own linens. No smoking/pets! Also available for ski weekends.

Weekly $750 (June 26-Labor Day) $420 (off-season)

MILLER'S GUEST HOUSE ON BURT LAKE   **(616) 238-4492**
JESS & PAM MILLER   VACATION HOME

One-of-a-kind spacious Burt Lake guest house. Recently built to exacting standards for our personal friends and family. Now available for up to 4 non-smoking guests. Includes complete kitchen, private sandy beach. Brilliant sunsets, quiet wooded atmosphere. Ideal for swimming, sailing, canoeing, bicycling. Friendly hosts. No pets.

Weekly $480

PINE DELIGHT BEACH COTTAGES   **(616) 238-7881**
                                               COTTAGES/EFFICIENCIES

These 10 units, from efficiencies to 3 bedroom cottages are furnished (linens provided) with fully equipped kitchens and color TV. Excellent sandy beach for good swimming. Boats and 100 ft. dock available for guests.

Weekly $200-$525

SHARON PRESSEY   SUMMER (906) 643-7733 • WINTER (407) 229-1599
                                               COTTAGES/HOME

Burt Lake, 2 and 3 bedroom cottages. 150' water frontage, 2 cottages 50' from water, one 200' away. One offers loft, one with fireplace, one with dishwasher. All have decks overlooking water, fully equipped kitchens, cable TV, gas grills & row boat. Bedding provided. Terrific walleye and bass fishing. Pets allowed. Open April-Oct.

Weekly $650-$750 ($375-$475 off-season)

CHEBOYGAN & MULLETT LAKE

ALGOMAH WHEELHOUSE INN   **(616) 627-3643**
EDMUND & SHIRLEY GIDDEY   BED & BREAKFAST

Next door to the Cheboygan Opera House, this elegant 2-story chalet (built in the early 1900's) features leaded glass cabinetry and oak woodwork. The 3 guest rooms offer sitting areas, down pillows and comforters, shared bath, A/C. Continental breakfast is served at a common table to encourage mingling and new friendships. No smoking.

Daily $35-$55

76

BIRCH LODGE CABINS (616) 627-5806
CABINS

On the Straits of Mackinac, these housekeeping cottages are fully furnished w/equipped kitchens, A/C, and color TV.

Call for Rates

LAKEWOOD COTTAGES (616) 238-7476
KEITH R. PHILLIPS COTTAGES

Clean comfortable 2-3 bedroom cottages located on Mullett Lake, with 750' of lake frontage. Screened porches, CATV, carpeted, fully equipped kitchens, showers, picnic tables, grills, boats and motors for rent. Buoys for private boats, swimming, fishing, and evening bonfires. Pets allowed. Available May-Sept.

Weekly $315-$375 Daily $50-$55

THE PINES OF LONG LAKE (616) 625-2121
COTTAGES

This year around resort offers 1-3 bedroom cottages. Two bedroom cabins face the lake, have 2 double beds and shared shower building (separate from the cabins), the 1 & 3 bedroom offer private showers. All have stoves, refrigerators, limited utensils, gas heat, blankets/pillows (bring linens). Bar and restaurant on premises. Pets allowed ($10 add'l).

Daily $40-$50 Weekly $185-$225

VEERY POINTE RESORT ON MULLETT LAKE (616) 627-7328
FRED SMITH & DEBBIE SOCHA COTTAGES/EFFICIENCIES

Lakefront cottages, open year around, all face the water, with docks. Fully furnished (except linens—linens available), includes microwave, CATV. Motel with efficiencies across from lake with beach privileges. Good fishing, x-country skiing, downhill skiing, skating and snowmobiling. No pets.

Weekly $200-$750

GAYLORD

HERITAGE HOUSE B&B (517) 732-1199
BED & BREAKFAST

Come to relax and enjoy the collection of old & new in this 100 year old farmhouse featuring 5 guest rooms. Close to downtown Gaylord. Full breakfasts and homemade treats served in dining area overlooking backyard.

Daily $55-$75

MICHIGAN COTTAGES • CHALETS • CONDOS • B&B'S

MARSH RIDGE   **(517) 732-6794**

HOTEL/TOWNHOUSES/CHALET(LODGE)

Each room features a unique decor and theme - some w/Jacuzzi, king sized beds, microwaves, refrigerators, and remote TVs. Townhouses with full kitchen, living room, bath, and bedroom downstairs (upstairs sleeping loft) and 2nd bath. The chalet/lodge features 4 bedrooms, 2 baths, fieldstone fireplace, full kitchen, deck , etc. Facilities feature swimming pool, shops & more! No pets!

	Hotel/Suites	Townhouses/Lodge
Weekend	$60-$150*	$140-$340**

* Based on Double Occupancy. ** Based on 6-10 guests. Call for additional info.

POINTES NORTH   **(517) 732-4493**

BETSY BERRY   **PRIVATE VACATION HOMES**

Eight private vacation homes (5 lakefront, 3 non-lakefront) for day, week or month rental. Sizes vary from 3 to 5 bedrooms (some include 2 car garage w/auto door opener). Each property features unique, tasteful decor — from spacious multi-level, sophisticated country to cozy, log cabin and chalet styling. All are set in secluded locations and come fully furnished and equipped including CATV and telephone. No pets.

Weekly $500-$1,200

Editor's Note: Reviewed in 1993. All lodgings very comfortable with good locations. Jessie's Landing was our favorite with its breathtaking view of the lake!

TREETOPS SYLVAN RESORT   **(800) 444-6711 • (517) 732-6711**

HOTEL/CHALET/EFFICIENCY

Standard hotel and deluxe suite accommodations (featuring whirlpool tub & wet bar) as well as efficiencies and chalets w/microwaves and kitchenettes. In the winter, Sylvan offers 14 downhill ski runs and 20 km. of groomed woodland x-country ski trails. Dining room, lounge, cafe on premises. Plus, outdoor/in-door heated pools and spa, whirlpool, weight room and more!

Call for Rates and Brochures

GRAYLING

BORCHER'S BED & BREAKFAST   **(517) 348-4921**

TINK & SHIRLEY HENRY/MARK & CHERI HUNTER   **BED & BREAKFAST**

The friendly hosts at Borcher's invite you to enjoy a unique river front experience! On the banks of the AuSable this charming inn, initially built in the early 1900's, is now fully restored. Six guest rooms feature twin and double beds (shared baths) and queen beds (private baths). Full breakfasts. Canoe rentals. Smoking permitted on porches. Open year around. No pets.

Daily $45-$75

78

HIGGINS LAKE

BIRCH LODGE
(517) 821-6261
COTTAGE RESORT

This 50 year old resort rests along the shores of Higgins Lake. The 17 cottages (1-3 bedroom/no kitchens) are simply furnished, maintained in good condition and sit in a semi-circle facing the water. Meals are included in the price. Open May-Oct.

Daily $70 (per adult; children rates less)
Weekly $430 (per adult; children rates less)

Editor's Note: The Lodge has developed a great reputation for preparing very tasty meals!

MORELL'S HIGGINS LAKE COTTAGE   (517) 821-6885 • (810) 733-0420
SANDY OR MARK MORELL   COTTAGE

Overlooking the south end of beautiful Higgins Lake, this immaculate, cozy cottage sits on a nicely wooded lot and is fully furnished w/equipped kitchen, two bedrooms and nursery. Cottage sleeps 5-6. Includes use of rowboat and a 4000 lb. hoist. No pets.

Weekly (Summer) $700
(After Labor Day thru June 17 — special rates.)

REZNICH'S COTTAGES
(517) 821-9282
COTTAGES

These three, two bedroom cottages on Higgins lake are clean, comfortable and offer tiled floors, privet bath, gas heat and equipped kitchen. BBQ, picnic table and rowboat included in rental price. All cottages are close to the water, one directly overlooks the lake and features knotty pine interior.

Weekly $350-$400

HOUGHTON LAKE

BEACHWOOD RESORT
(517) 366-5512
JUD & JOAN   COTTAGES

These 2 and 3 bedroom, fully furnished, log cabins feature fireplaces (wood provided), equipped kitchens (linens provided), private baths. Boat included with each cabin. Motors available. Shuffleboard, horseshoes, swings. Good swimming beach—great fishing! Owners in the process of renovating.

Weekly $300-$350   Daily $45 (and up)

MICHIGAN COTTAGES • CHALETS • CONDOS • B&B'S

THE CREST　　　　　　　　**(517) 366-7758 • (810) 363-9485**
　　　　　　　　　　　　　　　COTTAGES/EFFICIENCIES

These lakefront lodgings (3 cottages/3 efficiencies) feature nicely maintained, very clean facilities —inside and out! Furnishings in good condition and comfortable. All kitchens fully equipped and feature new wood grain countertops. Use of boat included. Tie-down and dock available for use. No pets.

Weekly　　　　$210-$450

Editor's Note: We visited these really cute, well maintained lodgings in 1993! They were clean and very nicely maintained!

DIETERICH'S RESORT　　　　　　　　　　**(517) 366-7655**
　　　　　　　　　　　　　　　　COTTAGES/EFFICIENCIES

These 2-3 bedroom cottages (sleeps 4-8) and efficiency units are completely furnished w/equipped kitchens, gas heat, private bathrooms w/showers. Most offer paneled walls, tile floors and include double bed, w/hide-a-bed or studio couch. Linens provided (bring your own towels). Swings, picnic tables, grills, fish cleaning house, shuffleboard, badminton, horseshoes on premises.

Call for Rates

DRIFTWOOD RESORT　　　　　　　**(517) 422-5229**
BOB & SHEILA BLESSING　　　　　　**COTTAGES**

Lakefront resort on 2 quite wooded acres on the north shore. Seven modern housekeeping cabins. Four are log cabins with fireplaces and microwaves. Cabins include porches with swings, color TV, full kitchens, carpeting. 14' aluminum boat, picnic table and grill. We have the ultimate playground with basketball, volleyball, horse shoes, swings, etc. Motor and paddle boat rental. Open all year. No pets.

Weekly $325-$515 (Call for daily rates.)

JACK'S HIDE-AWAY　　　　　　　**(517) 366-5822**
MARTHA & PHIL KEMMIS　　　　　　**COTTAGES**

A narrow, secluded dirt road on the north shore of the lake, takes you to Jack's Hide-Away which features almost 300 ft. of sandy beach. Each carpeted cottage is furnished and features equipped kitchens, bathroom/showers. Some offer queen size beds. Boats included in rental.

Call for Rates

80

Lagoon Resort & Motel
Don & Ellen Thomas

(517) 422-5761
Motel/Cottages

The resort offers motel units plus 2 & 3 bedroom cottages with full kitchens and double beds. It features 260' water frontage with a sandy beach, water slide, boat ramp, lighted playground, shuffleboard, and horseshoes court. Handicap access. Ice shanty, pontoon and water bike rentals available. Open all year. Daily rates available. No pets.

Weekly $375-$450

Lazy Days Assoc. Cottages

(810) 979-2819
Cottages

Near Tip-Up-Town site on the shores of Houghton Lake. Features 100 ft. sandy beach with 124 ft. dock. Cottages fully furnished and equipped. Kitchens include microwaves. Queen size beds, CATV. Boats available.

Call for Rates

Miller's Lakeshore Resort
Doug Miller

(810) 652-4240
Cottages/Chalet

Open all year. Good swimming, fishing, hunting, snowmobiling and ice fishing! New chalet with fireplaces. Modern lakefront housekeeping cottages. Large unit with fireplace. Boats with cottages. Motor rentals. Dockage. Safe sandy beach. Large playground. Grill and picnic tables. Ice shanty. On snowmobile trails. Located at Tip-Up Town, Zone 10. 306 Festival Drive. Visitors by approval. No pets.

Call for Rates

Morell's Maple Leaf Resort
Sandy & Don Morell

(517) 821-6885
Cottages

A large 3 bedroom and 2, 2 bedroom cottages located on north shore of Houghton Lake — are fully furnished w/equipped kitchens and baths. Cottages are heated and immaculate. Includes row boat. No pets.

Call for Rates

North Star Resort

(517) 422-4618
Cottages

On the north shore of the lake, in a relaxed wooded setting, these 6 cottages are open year around. Each sleeps 6 and features gas heat and equipped kitchens.

Weekly $300

MICHIGAN COTTAGES • CHALETS • CONDOS • B&B'S

PINE TREE RESORT   **(517) 366-7036 • (810) 469-0529**
PAM & DUNCAN HOGG   **COTTAGES**

On the east shore, these 1-3 bedroom cottages are fully furnished with equipped kitchens, bathroom w/showers, and carpeting. Boat included with rentals. Motors and paddle boats available.

Weekly $275-$425

SHADY VALLEY RESORT   **(517) 366-5403**
       COTTAGES

These fully furnished cottages feature equipped kitchens, CATV, carpeting and paneling in the bedrooms and living rooms. Some cottages offer screened porches. Newly built cottages available. Boat included in rental. Motors, pontoons, canoes, snowmobile rentals available. Playground, grills, lawn furniture, fire pit on beach. Handicap access. Pets allowed.

Weekly $325-$500   Daily $50-$85

Editor's Note: Visited in 1993. Clean and well maintained cabins on the water. We understand they built a new 4 bedroom and 2 bedroom cottage in 1994.

SONGER'S LOG CABINS   **(517) 366-5540**
AL & PAULINE SONGER   **COTTAGES**

Open year around, these clean and well maintained log cabins, located on the north shore of Houghton Lake with 150' lake frontage. Each two bedroom cabin features fully equipped kitchens, cable TV, private baths, screened porches and use of 14' boat. Several have natural fireplaces. Paddle boat, pontoon boat, tether ball, swimming and more! No pets (except for fall).

Weekly   *$450-$550 (summer)   Daily $65-$85 (winter)
*Rates reduced in winter

Editor's Note: Reviewed in 1993. Clean and cozy log cabins by the water — very nice!

SUN 'N SNOW RESORT   **(517) 422-5012**
       COTTAGES

On open grounds with 150' of sandy beach, this resort's cottages are fully carpeted and furnished with equipped kitchens, CATV, private baths and 14' boat. No linens. From 1-2 bedrooms sleeping 3-6. Resort feature game room w/pool table, fireplace and video games, playground area and more. Paddle boats, paddle boards, kayaks available. No pets.

Call for Rates

Editor's Note: This year around resort was very clean and nicely maintained when we visited in 1993!

Tradewinds Resort
Paul & Kim Carrick

(517) 422-5277
Cottages

This year around resort, offers carpeted, fully furnished cottages with equipped kitchens, private bath/showers, double beds, color CATV. Boats included w/ rentals. Motors and pontoon boats available. Facilities set on spacious grounds with sandy beach. Horseshoes, volleyball, shuffleboard, playground on premises. Provide your own linens and paper products. $125 deposit required.

Weekly $250-$400 (and up)   Daily $40-$65

West Shore Resort

(517) 422-3117
Cottages

Nicely maintained, clean and comfortable, these small 2 bedroom (sleep up to 6) cottages are fully furnished w/equipped kitchens. The cottage closest to the water is new, more spacious and offers attractive/ comfortable furnishings and nice view. Provide your own linens/towels during prime season (June-August). $100 deposit required. No pets.

Weekly $350-$646

Editor's Note: Reviewed in 1993. Mostly smaller but well maintained, clean cottages. The cottage nearest to the lake was good sized, comfortable and had a great view of the lake!

The Woodbine Villa

(517) 422-5349
Cottages

On 300' of sandy beach, these 2 bedroom log cottages are gas heated offer CATV, and are fully furnished with equipped kitchens. Includes use of playground, Aqua Swan boat, and paddle boats. Modern baths and saunas.

Call for Rates

LEWISTON

Gorton House
Lois & Tom Gorton

(517) 786-2764 • (313) 261-5347
Bed & Breakfast

Lakefront home on Little Wolf Lake. Antique themed rooms. Paddle boat, fishing boat and a 1920 regulation pool table available to all guests. Relax and enjoy the lake's view from the Gazeboed hot tub. Great area for x-country skiing, snowmobiling and golf! Full breakfast served on porch offering a panoramic view of the sunrise over Little Wolf. Gaylord 20 mile. 4 room with shared or private baths. Open May-March.

Daily $45-$75

LAKEVIEW HILLS COUNTRY INN RESORT & NORDIC SKI CENTER

(517) 786-2000
COUNTY INN/B&B

Each of its 14 rooms are furnished in authentic antiques (of different eras in American history) and feature private bath, CATV and individually controlled heating and A/C. Enjoy the beautifully groomed pro-croquet court, fitness center w/whirlpool, sauna and exercise equipment. Guests are served a full breakfast w/kitchen privileges. Relax in the great room, observatory, library or 165 foot porch. In the winter, enjoy 15 km. of cross-country ski trails!

Daily $79-$135

Editor's Note: Reviewed in 1993. Contemporary country styling, beautiful views in a secluded wooded setting. A professional croquet court adds an interesting touch. Great retreat!

REGION 3

REGION 3

After crossing the "Big Mac's" five mile span, you will see a place of remote beauty where the interstate highways are nonexistent and fast food restaurants and motel chains are hard to find. In their place are roads "off the beaten path" surrounded by natural beauty, family-run cottages, inns and cafes.

You will walk in the footsteps of our Forefathers and view the marvels of their ingenuity. You are entering a land of a unique combination of dense, unspoiled wilderness, wildlife of all types, streams and waterfalls, yet unnamed mountains and rock formations millions of years old.

You are entering the land of Hiawatha and Gitche Gumee.

ST. IGNACE TO SAULT STE. MARIE

COVERS: BARBEAU • CEDARVILLE • DRUMMOND ISLAND •
KINCHELOE • SUGAR ISLAND

St. Ignace is a community established in 1671 by the Ojibwa, Huron, and Ottawa tribes. The French Father, Jacques Marquette, was the first priest at the Mission of St. Ignace and became famous for his travels of the Great Lakes and Mississippi River. He is buried outside a 150 year old church which is now a museum in the Father Marquette State Park, located at the base of the Mackinac Bridge. Native American pow-wows are still held outside the mission church. Some are open to the public. There is much to do and see in and around St. Ignace besides Father Marquette's museum! Don't forget to see the Marquette Mission Park and the Museum of Ojibwa Culture and learn about Native Americans at the Straits of Mackinac. There is the "Car Corral" where there are toys, antique bikes, motor scooters, pedal cars and much more to see and buy. Take a ferry ride to Mackinac Island. If you are a walker, don't forget the famous Bridge walk on Labor Day and be a part of the thousands who walk the world's longest total suspension bridge.

Then, on to **Sault Ste. Marie** (meaning the Rapids of St. Mary), the oldest community in Michigan. It was first reached by Jesuit missionaries in 1641 and at that time was considered the Indians' summer gathering and fishing place. It is often referred to as the "Gateway to the North." Starting at the Sault, you will see the Great Rapids "white waters" as Lake Superior feeds into Lake Huron. The Soo Locks, an engineering marvel, were built in 1855 to raise or lower vessels up to 1,000 ft. in length through these "white waters". World famous, more tonnage passes through the Soo Locks than the Suez Cannel. After viewing the Soo Locks, walk the path to historic churches and homes. Take a boat trip through the Locks and marvel at the ingenuity of man. After viewing the Soo Locks, walk the path to historic churches and homes. See Mission Hill Cemetery, Tower of History and the Shipwreck Museum. Then on to a train ride, boat ride or relax on the beautiful sandy beach of Lake Superior. Golf and even casinos are not far away. In winter, enjoy snowmobiling, downhill and cross-country skiing, carnivals, skating and ice shows.

For more information on this area contact:

St. Ignace Area Chamber of Commerce
11 S. State Street
St. Ignace, MI 49781
(906) 643-8717 • (800) 338-6660

Sault Area Chamber of Commerce
2581 I 75 Business Spur
Sault St. Marie, MI 49783
(906) 632-3301 • (800) 647-2858

MICHIGAN COTTAGES • CHALETS • CONDOS • B&B'S

BARBEAU

CHANNEL VIEW RESORT (906) 647-7915
COTTAGES

Located 20 miles southeast of Sault Ste. Marie on the St. Mary's River, the resort offers spectacular views of long ships, and has excellent fishing. Cottages feature 2 bedrooms, double beds, heater, stove w/cookware, refrigerator, and TV. For more information write: Hi 51, Box 17A, Barbeau, MI 49710.

Weekly $165

RIVERVIEW TAXIDERMY & MARINE (906) 647-7211
CABINS

Located 23 miles southeast of the Soo Locks, all units overlook the St. Mary's River. Four housekeeping cabins include complete kitchen, 2 bedrooms (linens included). TV and screened porch, dock and boat ramp. Boat and motor rentals available. Great fishing. Smoking allowed. Pets allowed on a leash.

Weekly $170-$180 ($5 additional for each person)

CEDARVILLE

ISLAND VIEW RESORT, INC. (906) 484-2252
LARRY & JACKIE COTTAGES

Cottages have 2 and 3 bedrooms. Includes carpeting, showers, hot and cold water, gas heat and ranges, refrigerators, dishes and cooking utensils. All linens are furnished except towels and wash cloths. Fish cleaning house and freezer are provided. Playground equipment for children. Good swimming area. Great fishing for northern pike, yellow perch, large and small mouth bass, brown trout, muskie and several varieties of pan fish.

Weekly $315-$455

DRUMMOND ISLAND

CAPTAINS COVE RESORT (906) 493-5344
TRISH BRUGGER COTTAGES

These 9, 1 and 2 bedroom cottages sit in a wooded area on Gold Coast Shores in the heart of Potagannissing Bay. Newly remodeled, some are lakefront cabins w/fireplaces. All are completely furnished light housekeeping cottages with automatic heat, and bathroom w/showers. Boat included with each cabin. $100 refundable deposit required. No pets.

Weekly $270-$320 (based on 4 people)

WA-WEN RESORT (906) 493-5445 • (602) 746-2244
PHIL & MARCIA STITES CABINS
This 10 acre resort is located on a sheltered bay near the mouth of the Potagannissing River. Housekeeping cabins have 1-4 bedrooms. Kitchens fully equipped, electric stoves, bed linens and towels. Aluminum boat, an enclosed fish cleaning house, electric scaler and freezer available. Fishing supplies sold in tackle shop. Resort offers shuffleboard court, fire-pit, basketball/badminton court, picnic tables, charcoal grills and outdoor pool on premises.

Weekly $284 (based on 2 people) - $565 (based on 10 people)

KINCHELOE

EAGLE INN (906) 495-5228 • (906) 495-5810
GARY & TERRI TAYLOR INN
Two room suites offer A/C, CATV, refrigerators, direct dial phones and a continental breakfast. There are 27 suites available. Major credit cards are accepted. Reservations are appreciated. Open all year.

Daily $50 (1-2 Persons + Tax) - $80 (4 People + Tax)

ST. IGNACE

BALSAM'S RESORT (906) 643-9121
BETTY COTTAGES/MOTEL
At the Straits of Mackinac, 5 miles west of Big Mac, these "real log" cabins have fireplaces and are completely furnished with all kitchen equipment and linens (sorry, no heat). Private sandy beach, safe swimming, night bonfires, picnic, playground, shuffleboard, horseshoes, volleyball and badminton/croquet court. Nearby, there are 40 acres of woods full of beautiful gardens. Have served guests for over 65 years.

Daily $50-$80

SAULT STE. MARIE

CAPTAIN'S QUARTERS (906) 632-7075
CONDOS
Two bedroom condo completely furnished with nautical theme. Great view of ships. Three miles from Soo Locks and Kewadin Casino. Six golf courses nearby. Casino and golf packages available.

Call for Rates

MICHIGAN COTTAGES • CHALETS • CONDOS • B&B'S

THE WATER STREET INN   (800) 236-1904 • (906) 632-1900
PHYLLIS & GREG WALKER   BED & BREAKFAST

1900's Queen Anne home overlooking the St. Mary's River has stained glass windows, Italian marble fireplaces, and original woodwork. A wide wraparound porch for watching passing freighters promises a special visit whatever the season. North country breakfast served in an elegant dining room. Only B&B in Sault Ste. Marie. Emphasis is on hospitality and tranquillity. Walking distance from the locks and fine restaurants. 4 rooms.

Daily $70-$95

SUGAR ISLAND

BENNETT'S LANDING   (906) 632-2987
                                            CABINS

This fishing resort located on the shores of Big Lake George, has been newly remodeled including a new general store. The cabins offer linens, and have a full kitchen, heat, handicap access and a boat. They rent boats, motors, bait and also have propane for RVs. Open May 1-Oct. 15.

Weekly $225   Daily $50

NELSON'S RESORT   (906) 632-6901
                                            CABINS

Located in East Portage, 3 miles from the Soo Locks on the St. Mary's River. Overlooks Canada and the Laurantian Mountains. These newly remodeled housekeeping cabins offer linens and use of boat (motor rental available). The resort features boat ramp and dock, live bait, fish cleaning station, and fish freezing facility. Take advantage of the running season for pink and hump-back salmon.

Call for Rates

BREVORT • PARADISE

COVERS: HULBERT • TROUT LAKE

A s you travel along M 123, stop at **Hulbert** and plan a trip on the Tom Sawyer River Boat and Paul Bunyon Timber Train, or the Toonerville Trolley and River Boat. Both offer 4-1/2 hour round trips to the Tahquamenon Falls with commentary on fauna, flora, points of interest and wildlife. Then on to Paradise, only 10 miles from the second largest waterfall east of the Mississippi River. It is sometimes called Little Niagara, for here lies Tahquamenon Falls in all its glory. Not far away is Whitefish Point and its Great Lakes Shipwreck Museum. This is where you will find the "Graveyard of the Great Lakes" and the first Lighthouse of Lake Superior. A moment of silence for our most recent loss, The Edmund Fitzgerald, which sank in 1975.

Sorry — no Chamber of Commerce available

BREVORT

CLEARWATER RESORT HOTEL   **(800) 638-6371 • (906) 292 5506**
AND CONDOMINIUM   CONDO & HOTEL

Just 22 miles west of the Mackinac Bridge. These beautiful, clean and quiet condos face Lake Michigan. Only a few years old, they offer 2-3 bedrooms w/fully equipped kitchens and walkout decks Most offer dishwasher, microwaves, and phone. Towels and sheets provided. Resort includes indoor pool, racquetball, sauna, dining room, and lounge.

Call for Rates

HULBERT

HULBERT LAKE LODGE   **(906) 876-2324**
GREG & MARGE CURTIS   CABINS

Five heated log cabins plus 8 duplexes situated 1/4 mile into the forest have 1-3 bedrooms (one w/fireplace). Furnished but no kitchen facilities. Main lodge offers hearty home cooked breakfasts and dinners. Boats, motors, bait available. Come see the beautiful fall colors. While you are here, do some fantastic snowmobiling, ice fishing and x-country skiing.

Weekly $266-$525   Daily rates available

MICHIGAN COTTAGES • CHALETS • CONDOS • B&B'S

SNO-SHU INN   **(906) 876-2324**
GREG & MARGE CURTIS   **CABINS/INN**

Cozy housekeeping cabins and apartments are fully furnished with kitchen and private bath/showers. Lodging at the Inn accommodates up to 20 people. Fantastic snowmobiling from your door. Heated workshops. Bring your horse and ride miles of wooded trails—stabling available.

Daily $45-$70 (cottage/efficiency units) and $150-$240 (inn)

PARADISE

LAKEVIEW CABINS & THE OLD MILL   **(906) 492-3907 • (906) 492-3368**
CAFETERIA & BUFFET (BOB & RENEE BERRY)   **CABINS**

Centrally located between Whitefish Point and Tahaquamenon Falls, in a secluded birch grove overlooking the sandy beach and bay (only 1/4 mile from town). All cabins fully supplied housekeeping units. Safe swimming, BBQ grills, tables, firepits, play equipment and toys for the kids. The "Old Mill" is across the street and features home cooking.

Daily $40-$75 (Based on 2 people)

MILE CREEK CABINS   **(906) 492-3211**
DAN & LINDA SMYKOWSKI   **CABINS**

Modern, authentic log cabins (studio to 2 bedrooms) are clean, carpeted, comfortable and fully furnished including linens. All cabins overlook Lake Superior and provide a magnificent view in a white birch setting. Each features color TV, fireplace (wood provided). Great swimming on private beach. Centrally located to Tahquamenon Falls and Whitefish Point. X-country ski and snowmobile right from your door. Open year around. Pets allowed but must be kept under control.

Daily* $29-$49 (Based on 2 people)
* Cash discount available.

TROUT LAKE

TROUT LAKE RESORT   **(906) 569-3810**
                                                   CABINS

Just 45 minutes from the Mackinac Bridge, these clean comfortable cabins overlook Trout Lake. Each cabin has a fully equipped kitchenette with microwave, and color TV. Fishing boat is included.

Call for Rates

92

TWIN CEDARS RESORT — **(906) 569-3209**
COTTAGES/MOTEL

Small resort located in the Upper Peninsula—a 35 minute drive from St. Ignace, on beautiful Frenchman's Lake. Cozy, two bedroom cottages and <u>plush</u> motel accommodations. Reduced rates in <u>portions</u> of off-season in <u>these</u> rooms. Well established. Extras too numerous to list! For complete information, please phone/write. <u>Many</u> regular guests, therefore, calling for info. is recommended. Address: 95 Trout Lake, Michigan 49793

Call for Rates

GRAND MARAIS TO GULLIVER

COVERS: BLANEY PARK • CURTIS

Grand Marais is the "Eastern Gateway" to the Pictured Rocks National Lakeshore. This lovely, unspoiled village offers it all — ladyslippers and trillium, white-tailed deer, black bear, Canadian lynx, moose and — even our own bald eagle resides in this beautiful Upper Peninsula wilderness. As might be expected, boating, fishing, hunting, skiing, and snowmobiling are "the thing to do" in this area. The Grand Marais Historical Museum, Pictured Rocks Maritime Museum, and the AuSable Lighthouse are some of its attractions. But, of course while you are here, you must be sure to explore their many scenic overlooks including the Log Slide, Munising Falls, Sable Falls and don't forget the unforgettable Tahquamenon Falls and the beautiful Pictured Rocks along Gitche Gumee (Lake Superior)! This area is a photographer's dream—**bring your camera!**

If you're in the **Gulliver** area, be sure to enjoy a casual meal at *Fisher's Old Deerfield Inn* which features an informal log cabin atmosphere and quaint dining room!

For more information about events and activities contact:

Grand Marais Chamber of Commerce
P.O. Box 139
Grand Marais, MI 49839
(906) 494-2766

BLANEY PARK

CELIBETH HOUSE   **(906) 283-3409**
ELSA R. STROM   BED & BREAKFAST

This lovely home on 85 acres overlooks Lake Anne Louise. Rooms are clean, spacious, and comfortably furnished. Guests may enjoy the cozy living room, a quiet reading room, a comfortably furnished front porch, and a spacious deck. Continental breakfast. No smoking. 8 rooms.

Daily $40-$50 sgl. $45-$55 dbl.

BLANEY COTTAGES   **(906) 283-3163**
                                                  COTTAGES

11 Cottages, 1-3 bedrooms feature fireplaces, gas heat, color TV and all new furniture. Free coffee, donuts and paper each morning. Features include: special rates to seniors, smoking/non-smoking cabins, and a new game room. Picnic area includes gas grills and tables. X-country skiing and snowmobiling in the winter. Nearby is Seney National Wildlife Refuge, Pictured Rocks, Tahquamenon Falls and more. Open all year.

Call for Rates

CURTIS

MANILAK RESORT   **(800) 586-6690 • (800) 586-3285**
                                             CHALETS & RANCHES

Located 2 miles N. of Curtis, Manilak offers both chalet and ranch style homes (sleep 1-12 people). All are carpeted with wood burning fireplaces, full baths, fully equipped kitchens, linens, charcoal grills, picnic tables and decks overlooking the Manistique Lake. Includes use of rowboat. Activity area with basketball, volleyball, horseshoes, recreation room with sauna and spa recently added! Scenic attractions are all within an hours drive. Open year around. No pets.

Weekly $450-$1,100

GRAND MARAIS

HILLTOP MOTEL & CABINS   **(906) 494-2331**
                                                  CABINS/MOTEL

Five cozy motel units (2 w/kitchenettes), 5 completely furnished housekeeping cabins. All include gas heaters, showers and TV. Outdoor fireplace, grills, picnic and play area. Also includes 9 hole mini golf.

Call for Rates

94

THE RAINBOW LODGE   **(906) 658-3357**
CABINS

All new, modern cabins! Full housekeeping services. Each cabin sleeps up to 6 and features a complete kitchen. Linens are furnished — all you need to do is come! Three day minimum stay required. Call to confirm rates.

Weekly $275 (approx.)

GULLIVER

FISCHER'S OLD DEERFIELD   **(906) 283-3169**
COTTAGES

Located on the shore of Gulliver Lake, 21 up-to-date, clean lakeside motel units & housekeeping cottages w/private, shallow, sandy beach. Set on 10 acres of tall pines, each unit has pine paneled walls, bath w/shower, and automatic heat. Stroll among the well groomed grounds. On the premises there are wooded nature trails, restaurant, lounge, gift shop, and also a fish cleaning cabin. Eat at Fisher's Old Deerfield Inn, with informal log cabin atmosphere and two quaint dinning rooms. Open May through November.

Call for Rates

AUTRAIN • GARDEN • MANISTIQUE
MUNISING • WETMORE

Just north of **Manistique** you will find Palms Books State Park where you will see one of the most unusual water sites in the Upper Peninsula. Take a wooden raft out to the middle of crystal clear Kitch-iti-kipi (Bring Spring) and watch as more than 23 million gallons of water daily erupt from the lake's bottom.

While in **Garden,** visit the Gayette Historical Townsite and take a walking tour through the well preserved example of a 19th century company town. For you fishermen, stop at either Big Bay de Noc or Little Bay de Noc. Why? Because it is rated in USA Today as one of the top ten walleye fishing spots in the country. With nearly 200 miles of shoreline, the bay hosts perch, smallmouth bass, northern pike, rainbow trout, salmon, and fishing tournaments. Here also are uncongested golf courses and golf tournaments. Even a Las Vegas style gambling casino called "Chip-in-Casino" is found here. In the winter there are pow wows and sled dog races. In **Munising**, take a cruise along the shores of the world famous Pictured Rocks — Miner's Castle, Battleship Rock, Indian Head, Lovers' Leap, Colored Caves, Rainbow Cave and

AUTRAIN • GARDEN • MANISTIQUE
MUNISING • WETMORE

(continued...)

Chapel Rock, for these can only be seen from the water. Visiting **Au Train,** you will walk in the footsteps of Hiawatha for, according to Longfellow, here lies his home. Es'ca'naw'ba, from the Indian Eshkonabang, means flat rock. Longfellow's "Hiawatha" tells of the rushing Escanaba River, sometimes referred to as the land of the Red Buck. While in Au Train, for good family dining at very reasonable prices, check out *Dog Patch Restaurant.*

For additional information on events and activities in the area, contact:

Schoolcraft County Chamber of Comm. Alger Chamber of Commerce
P.O. Box 72   115 E. Munising Avenue
Manistique, MI 49854   Munising, MI 49862
(906) 341-5010   (906) 387-2138

AUTRAIN

COLEMAN'S PARADISE RESORT   **(906) 892-8390**
BILL & MICHELLE COLEMAN   **COTTAGES**
Located on the west side of AuTrain Lake, this resort offers 13 bedroom cottages. Each private cottage is completely furnished. Three bedroom cottages have fireplaces. Large deck overlooks sandy beach. Great swimming. Playground, w/horseshoes, volleyball, badminton, basketball. General store & bait shop. Boats included (motors available).

Weekly $270-$500

DANA'S LAKESIDE RESORT   **(906) 892-8333**
BARRY & LINDA CLEARY   **COTTAGES**
Heated 2-3 bedroom housekeeping cottages are 3 miles S. of M-28 on the west side of AuTrain Lake. The resort offers sandy beach, fiberglass boats (motors available), lighted boat dock, screened in fish cleaning house. Shuffleboard and horseshoes. Recreation building offers pool table, pinball, video games, air hockey, juke box & more. Washer and dryer are available.

Call for Rates

FOREST VIEW RESORT   **(906) 892-8225**
STEVE & DONNA CONGER   **COTTAGES**
On the west side of AuTrain, enjoy excellent fishing in Lake Superior. Seven completely furnished, 3 bedroom, housekeeping cottages (bring towels). Resort offers laundry facilities, sauna, recreation room, large play area. Boat

96

Forest View Resort (continued...)

included (motors available). Sandy beach, nightly campfires, easy access to trails for mountain biking, hiking and x-country skiing on well groomed trails. Snowmobile from your very own cottage.

Weekly $280-$375 (approx.)

Harrington Harbor   **(906) 892-8123 • (419) 855-8248**
Cabins

These 2-3 bedroom log housekeeping cabins are located on the west shore of Au Train Lake. Private sandy beach w/raft, playground, badminton, horseshoes, volleyball, and more. Also features a sauna and fish house. Includes boat.

Call for Rates

Northwoods Resort   **(906) 892-8114**
Gwen & Pam McCollum   **Cottages**

Located in Hiawatha National Forest, with easy access to all major highways, a paved roadway will bring you to this resort. Set on Au Train Lake, the resort offers good walleye, northern pike, and perch fishing. These two and three bedroom cottages, w/housekeeping, are fully equipped, and heated.

Weekly $250-$375 (approx.)

Pinewood Lodge Bed & Breakfast   **(906) 892-8300**
Jerry & Jenny Krieg   **Bed & Breakfast**

Log-styled inn, open year around, on 350' of private beach. Decor of 8 rooms from antiques to log. Relax on front porch, lakeside deck or sandy beach. Enjoy hot tub and sauna. Full breakfast served overlooking Lake Superior. Hiawatha National Forest, Pictured Rocks, x-country skiing and snowmobile trails nearby.

Daily $75-$110

Editor's Note: This is a most inviting B&B! Wonderful country-styled rooms gives a rustic, woodsy feel with all the "new" conveniences! Jenny's own skillful hands make many of the crafts decorating these rooms! See our review in this edition!

GARDEN

The Summer House   **(906) 644-2457**
Jan and Phil McCotter   **Bed & Breakfast**

Built in 1880, this two-story Colonial Revival home has been restored and decorated in Victorian style. It is located on the picturesque Garden Peninsula, just 7 miles from Fayette State Historical Park. Enjoy swimming, hunting, fishing, hiking and snowmobile trails. Explore area antique shops or just relax! 5 rooms.

Daily $35-$75 dbl.

MANISTIQUE

SEQUOYA RESORT   **(906) 341-5391**
LODGE/CABINS

On the southeast side of Indian Lake on Sunset Beach. These 2,3 & 6 bedroom cabins are situated on 10 wooded acres with 350 ft. beach. Fully heated, equipped kitchens, private baths (bring towels/linens). Shuffleboard, horseshoes, picnic tables and grills. Use of 14 ft. boat and ice shanty per unit. Pontoon, paddleboat and motors available. A $75 non-refundable deposit required. Open year around.

Weekly $325-$800 (Daily and weekly off season rates available.)

MUNISING

CAMEL RIDERS RESORT   **(906) 573-2319**
CABINS

Four fully carpeted, heated, fully furnished housekeeping cabins (2-3 bedrooms) open all year, on the "Chain of Lakes" in a wilderness setting. All bathrooms with modular showers, glass doors and vanities. Knotty pine interiors. Bring towels. Great sandy swimming beach, 2 docks, and 14' aluminum boat. Motors, gas, oil, paddle boat, and canoe available. Log cabin restaurant overlooks the lake rated one of best in the U.P. Full menu.

Weekly $330-$475 (based on 4 people) Daily $30

WHITE FAWN LODGE   **(906) 573-2949**
CABINS/MOTEL

In the heart of Hiawatha National Forest, White Fawn Lodge cabins include TV, microwave, refrigerator, coffee machines. Lodge offers room suites, hot tub and community building. Enjoy fishing, hunting, hiking, trails, waterfalls. Located 2 hours from the Mackinaw Bridge.

Call for Rates

WETMORE

CABIN FEVER RESORT   **(906) 573-2372**
RICK & COLLEEN JOHNSON   **LOG CABINS**

On 10 acres, these log cabins are fully carpeted and completely furnished with log furniture. Each has housekeeping facilities for 1-6 people (1-3 bedrooms), with fully equipped kitchen and private bath w/shower. Game room. Use of boat included. Excellent snowshoeing, x-country ski and snowmobile trails.

Weekly $240 (and up)

REGION 4

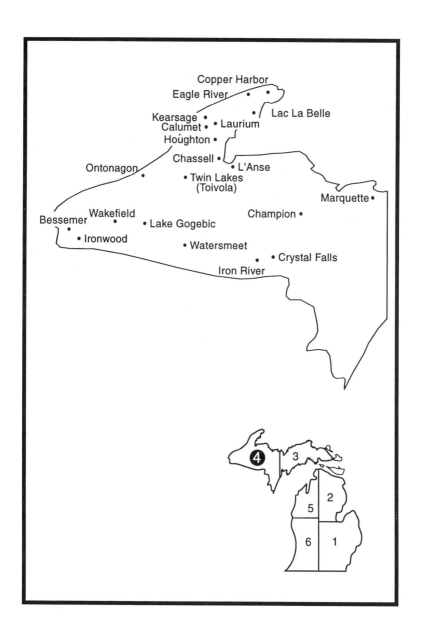

REGION 4

Welcome to this region of deep wilderness. Here is the beauty of nature, cascading waterfalls, panoramas of forest wilderness. A lake set in a sea of red, yellow and orange painted by fall leaves, set deep between and surrounded by mountains. A narrow peninsula that jets into Lake Superior and dares its mighty force and yet so lovely that the wealthy have built their summer homes here. A wilderness so complete that some areas can only be reached by hiking, biking or backpacking. You will see hues of red in the sand as Lake Superior sculptures the dunes along its shores. An area so breathtaking, poets have written about it. Lakes so crystal clear you can see the fish in their leisurely swim.

Take a fishing cruise on Lake Superior and catch that "big one". Salmon fishing here is comparable only to fishing in the ocean. Take any tour by boat or by land to see the mines and the wonder of this area. Sop and eat at one of their many fine restaurants.

In the winter, all you skiers, come to the mountain ranges that receive 250 inches of snow yearly. And, if you dare — and what skier is not — go *ski flying*. Ski flying is ski jumping but much higher, much longer and definitely more challenging!

You have now seen Michigan's Upper Peninsula!
You will long remember it — and you will soon return!

MARQUETTE THROUGH KEWEENAW PENINSULA TO SILVER CITY

COVERS: CALUMET • CHAMPION • CHASSELL • COPPER HARBOR •
EAGLE RIVER • HOUGHTON • KEARSARGE • LAC LA BELLE • L'ANSE •
LAURIUM • ONTONAGON (PORCUPINE MTNS. & LAKE OF THE CLOUDS) •
TWIN LAKES (TOIVOLAS)

Marquette, one of the oldest cities in the Upper Peninsula, was initially founded in the 1840's by French settlers to serve the iron-ore mining and lumber industries. Visitors to the area will enjoy the 328-acre Presque Isle Park with its extensive cross country and hiking trails or its International Food Festival, in July, hosted by Northern Michigan University. There are plenty of historic sites and outdoor activities to fill your day. As you leave Marquette for Copper Country, you'll want to stop at the *Mt. Shasta Restaurant* in the **Champion/Michigamme** area where several scenes from the 1950's movie, *Anatomy of a Murder,* were filmed. Here you'll find pictures of Jimmy Stewart, Lee Remick and other cast members adorning the walls.

Thrill to a genuine underground adventure—The Arcadian Copper Mines not far from **Houghton/Hancock**. Take a tour and see the geological wonders created eons ago deep inside the earth. Here, too, is a mecca for rock hounds. Then on to the Quincy Mine Hoist (the Nordberg Hoist), the largest steam-powered mine hoist ever manufactured. Not only is the hoist of great interest, but so is the lore of the Quincy Mining Company. You'll have to visit the area to learn more about it!

In **Calumet,** visit Coppertown USA's Visitor Center. It tells the story of mines, communities and the people of the Keweenaw Peninsula. Visit Fort Wilkins located on the shores of the Lake Superior. Comb through the gemstone strewn beaches to Jacob's Falls. In **Kearsarge,** stop at the "Last Place on Earth" and see the unusual but elegant spoons hand carved from local woods. Theater buffs must stop at the Calumet Theatre and walk with the "Greats" — Bernhardt, Fairbanks, and Sousa. While visiting the area, you'll want to stop at *The Old Country House* just two miles north of Calumet known for its fresh Lake Superior fish, prime rib and homemade bread!

Copper Harbor, at the tip of the peninsula, is a village where everything is less than four blocks away. Stop at the Laughing Loon Gift Shop and from there get a tour into the countryside to view the untouched, towering Estivant Pines. Before the tour, stop for breakfast at the *Pines Restaurant* and taste one of "Red" Twardzik's cinnamon rolls—a local institution — or *Johnson's Bakery* for great rolls and coffee. The aroma alone from these tasty places will add 10 lbs.! Of course, your trip to Copper Harbor is not complete until you dine at the *Keweenaw Mountain Lodge*. Here in this wilderness setting you will find cuisine at its finest! Take a boat trip to Isle Royale National

MARQUETTE THROUGH KEWEENAW PENINSULA TO SILVER CITY

(continued...)

Park, a roadless land of wildlife, unspoiled forests, refreshing lakes, and rugged scenic shores. You will find massive waves exploding on a rugged coastline, lighthouses, rolling hills, thimbleberries, vast pines and hardwood forests, a unique culture and accent. Best of all, you can view both the spectacular sunset and sunrise no matter where you are. Here is vacation land at its very best.

For additional information about these areas, contact:

Keweenaw Tourism Counsel
1197 Calumet Ave., Calumet, MI 49913
(906) 337-4579 • (800) 338-7982 (out-of-Michigan)

CALUMET

BOSTROM-JOHNSON HOUSE   **(906) 337-4651**
CURT & PAT JOHNSON   **BED & BREAKFAST**
A large Victorian era residence features 4 spacious guest rooms furnished in antiques. Guests will find a friendly, cheerful home within walking distance of Calumet. X-country ski and groomed snowmobile trails nearby. Children welcome. 4 rms/2 baths. Library open for reading or visiting at all times. There is tea and coffee available all day and a full breakfast every morning.

Daily $50   Double

CALUMET HOUSE B&B   **(906) 337-1936**
GEORGE & ROSE CHIVSES   **BED & BREAKFAST**
Located in the Keweenaw Peninsula and built in 1895, this B&B features original woodwork, upright piano and antique furniture. Breakfast is served in the formal dining room which has an original butler's pantry. Guests can view television in the drawing room by a cozy fire with their evening tea. No smoking or pets. Adults only.

Daily $25-$30

THE THIMBLEBERRY INN   **(906) 337-1332**
                                                                              BED & BREAKFAST
This turn of the century home has a porch and spacious yard. Two sitting rooms with fireplaces, large cheerful dining room with lace curtains, where a full

THE THIMBLEBERRY INN (continued...)
breakfast is served each morning. Six rooms share 2 full baths. Each room has a sink, some of antique marble. Master Card and Visa accepted. Open year around. They will be glad to help plan your exploration of the Keweenaw Peninsula.

Call for Rates

CHAMPION

MICHIGAMME LAKE LODGE B&B
(800) 358-0058
BED & BREAKFAST

In a wilderness setting rests this exclusive, historic grand pine lodge overlooking Lake Michigamme. Many antiques and original Indian carpets throughout. Spacious rooms are individually decorated, some featuring log-styled furniture. Dramatic 2-1/2 story stone fireplace and hand hewn stairway grace the entrance. Open May-Oct. 8 rooms w/private baths.

Daily $80-$125

Editor's Note: This is an exceptional and unique lodging—wonderful atmosphere in a natural setting. Great fishing area! See our review in this edition.

CHASSELL

THE HAMAR HOUSE
(906) 523-4670
BED & BREAKFAST

Built in circa 1903, this turn-of-the-century Victorian, set on spacious grounds, features 2 rooms with adjoining sunroom and 3 rooms with shared bath. Children welcome. Enjoy the 3/5 size playhouse. Parking for snowmobiles and trailers. Close to shops, lakefront, ski/snowmobile trails. Open year around. Check or cash only.

Call for Rates

HELMICK'S LOG CABINS
(906) 523-4591
MARYANN HELMICK
CABINS
3 heated, lakeside cabins. One large room (sleeps 4). Private baths. Equipped kitchen includes refrigerator, stove, pots/pans, dishes, utensils. Porches face the lake. Boats available. Open June 1-Oct. 1. No pets.

Weekly $180

MICHIGAN COTTAGES • CHALETS • CONDOS • B&B'S

LOG COTTAGE (617) 837-5960
MARCIA LITTLEFIELD COTTAGE

This log cottage home is situated on Half Moon Beach near Chassell. It features one bedroom, loft, complete kitchen, sauna and fishing boat.

Call for Rates

MANNINEN'S CABINS (906) 523-4135(W) • (906) 334-2518 (S)
CABINS

The 7 housekeeping cabins, located on 60 acres of land, are very accessible. The cabins, on Otter Lake (well known for outstanding fishing), come with boats. Open May 15-Oct. 1.

Call for Rates

NORTHERN LIGHT COTTAGES (906) 523-4131
GARY & MARGE WICKSTROM COTTAGES

Three fully furnished cottages on Chassell Bay. Two bedrooms sleep up to 6, bed linens provided. Sandy beach, swimming, fishing, docking space. Boats, sauna and campfire site are available.

Weekly $195 and up

PALOSAARI'S ROLLING ACRES B&B (906) 523-4947
CLIFF & EVEY PALOSAARI BED & BREAKFAST

Operating Dairy Farm since the 1920's! Visit the barn and watch the milking or help feed the baby calves. It is centrally located and offers three comfortable, cozy rooms with shared bath. Enjoy a full country breakfast in this "home away from home." Open year round. No smoking/pets. Snowmobile trails, swimming and hiking nearby.

Call for Rates

Editor's Note: Charming owners and unique "operating dairy farm" B&B. The rooms here are very comfy! A great place to bring the kids. They'll enjoy the farm and so will you! See our review in this edition.

104

COPPER HARBOR

BELLA VISTA MOTEL & COTTAGES
EARL LAMPPA
(906) 289-4213
COTTAGES/MOTEL

Eight cottages, in Copper Harbor, overlook beautiful Lake Superior. They have kitchenettes, color CATV. Fish off the dock, or if you prefer, boats are available. Open May to Mid-October.

Weekly $180-$190   Daily $34-$40

BERGH'S WATERFRONT RESORT
HOWARD & PHYLLIS BERGH
(906) 289-4234
COTTAGES

These comfortable housekeeping cottages are fully equipped. They include showers, dishes and linens, also boat w/dock available. Resort overlooks harbor near Copper Harbor Marina.

Call for Rates

LAKE FANNY HOOE RESORT
ALAN & GRACE CATRON
(906) 289-4451
COTTAGES/MOTEL

Four units on the lake with 3, 1-2 bed cottages and a lake front motel. Units have private balconies, kitchenettes, private baths, and some gas fireplaces. Wooded campsites w/ trout stream. Laundromat, clubhouse, sauna on premises. Boat included. Canoes available.

Weekly $325-$450

HARBOR LANE COTTAGES
JIM & JANET SHEA
(407) 639-2676 • (906) 289-4211
COTTAGES

Four log cabins, a century old, offer natural surroundings on Lake Superior. Completely furnished, including linens. Cozy fireplaces w/firewood, and lakeside decks. You can fish off your deck or boat. Fishing guide service, motor and canoe rental available. Within walking distance from Copper Harbor. 50% non-refundable deposit. Pets allowed for an additional $10.

Weekly $325-$450

KEWEENAW MOUNTAIN LODGE
(906) 289-4403
CABINS/LODGE

Surrounded by acres of primeval forest land, this framed mountain lodge is located in the Keweenaw Peninsula. Lodge features gracious dining room, cocktail lounge and golf course. Most cabins offer fireplaces, comfortable living areas with private baths and 1-3 bedrooms (no kitchens).

Daily $54-$69

Editor's Note: Comfortable lodgings, beautifully landscaped in a wilderness setting with all the modern conveniences. The restaurant serves well prepared meals! See our review in this edition.

EAGLE RIVER

THE EAGLE'S NEST

(906) 337-4441
BED & BREAKFAST

Built as a mining captain's home in 1858, this stately home is on 20 secluded acres. Victorian living room, stained glass windows and period furnishing. Three guest rooms share baths. Full breakfast. One mile from Lake Superior. Open year around. Adults only. VISA/MC accepted.

Call for Rates

EAGLE RIVER LAKESHORE CONDOMINIUMS
DANIEL JACKSON

(906) 337-4649
CONDOMINIUMS

Furnished recreational condominiums for sale or rent. Choose 1 or 2 bedroom units on Lake Superior's rugged Keweenaw Peninsula. All units with decks or porches over looking the Lake. Over 500 ft. of private swimming beach. Close to snowmobile trails, nature and pristine northwoods wilderness.

Call for Rates

EAGLE RIVER'S SUPERIOR VIEW
PAUL OR CURTNEY

(906) 482-7102
VACATION HOME

Three bedroom vacation home overlooking Lake Superior and the Sand Dunes. Sleeps 10 comfortably, 1-1/2 baths, fully equipped kitchen, modern decor. Linens provided. Fireplace, washer/dryer. Full screened porch. Excellent snowmobiling, skiing, swimming beach and play area. Pets and Smoking allowed. Call for free brochure.

Weekly $475 (winter/summer)   Daily $75 (winter only)

HOUGHTON

CHARLESTON HOUSE BED & BREAKFAST

(906) 482-7790
BED & BREAKFAST

This home replicates the homes of Charleston, S. Carolina with double piazza, formal gardens and gazebo. Antique period furniture with queen canopy beds, and twin beds, sitting room with fireplace, central air, color TV, direct dial phones. There are 3 rooms with private and semi-private baths. A buffet breakfast is served every morning. Situated on Houghton's waterfront and near bathing beach, boat docks and boardwalks. Bicycles available. Children 12 and over welcome. Major credit cards accepted. No smoking or pets.

Call for Rates

106

KEARSARGE

BELKNAP'S GARNET HOUSE   **(906) 337-5607**
BED & BREAKFAST
Enjoy the huge porch and 3 acres of this beautiful mining captain's Victorian home. Unchanged throughout the 1900's, it still has the original fireplaces, fur room, leaded/beveled glass pantries, fixtures, woodwork, and servants quarters. Each room is decorated with Victorian theme. 5 rooms/2 shared baths. Full breakfast. Open mid-June through mid-September. Adults only. VISA/MC accepted.

Call for Rates

LAC LA BELLE

LAC LA BELLE RESORT   **(906) 289-4293**
SANDY   **CABINS**
A quiet place at the end of the road. Basic fishing/snowmobiling, camp 35 miles from anywhere! Five cabins (3 on water) 1 and 2 bedrooms. Gas heat, showers, fully equipped kitchens, linens, dock space. Rental boats available. Convenience store and gift shop with limited groceries, beer and wine. Gas on dock and road. Access to Lake Superior via Mendota Canal.

Weekly $200 and up   Daily $40 and up

L'ANSE

THE BUNGALOW BED & BREAKFAST   **(906) 524-7595**
LORA WESTBERG & PAT OSTERMAN   **BED & BREAKFAST**
This bungalow sits serenely 40 ft. above the shores of Lake Superior in a densely wooded area. It is Henry Ford's summer home where he entertained many visitors including Thomas Edison and Harvey Firestone. 8 rooms.

Daily $65-$85

LAURIUM

KEWEENAW HOUSE BED & BREAKFAST   **(906) 337-4822**
BED & BREAKFAST
Elegant 6 bedroom home built in 1898 for a prominent family. Completely renovated and tastefully decorated with both old and the new. Features queen size beds in most rooms, comforters and antiques. Five rooms, 3 with two piece bath. Continental breakfast. Private living room, TV, kitchen area and

MICHIGAN COTTAGES • CHALETS • CONDOS • B&B'S

KEWEENAW HOUSE BED & BREAKFAST (continued...)
microwave available on request. Comfort and friendly small town charm is the essence of this lovely home. Children must sleep with parents. Open year round. No smoking or pets.

Daily $35-$50

LAURIUM MANOR INN   **(906) 337-2549**
                                                            BED & BREAKFAST

Built in 1905, this opulent 13,000 sq ft. antebellum style mansion has 41 rooms (including a ballroom), 5 fireplaces, hand painted murals and gilded leather wall covering. This elegant mansion offers 10 bedrooms, 6 private bath, 4 shared bath, king and queen size beds. Take a tour of this mansion and relive the unforgettable wealth that once was Copper Country. No smoking. No pets.

	Winter	**Summer**
Daily	$59-$89 pvt. bath	$69-$109 pvt. bath
	$49 sh. bath	$49 sh. bath

Editor's Note: Elegant and inviting, this is a premiere Victorian styled B&B. See our review in this edition!

WONDERLAND MOTEL & CABINS   **(906) 337-4511**
                                                            CABINS/MOTEL

These lodgings offer 10 units, 6 housekeeping cabins & 4 motel units. Clean quiet and comfortable.

Call for Rates

MARQUETTE

WHITEFISH LODGE   **(906) 343-6762**
KAREN HART & STEVE PAWIELSKI   **LODGE/COTTAGES**

A quiet retreat in the U.P. northwoods on the picturesque Laughing Whitefish River. All new, 2 and 3 bedroom lodgings, each completely furnished throughout including kitchens, bedrooms (queen beds) and baths. Enjoy our outdoor decks, mountain bikes, excellent walking and biking trails from door. Five minutes from Lake Superior and close to Pictured Rocks. Open year-round — on the snowmobile trail and close to x-country ski trails. 17 miles east of Marquette and 21 miles west of Munising, off M28.

Weekly $315-$525

Editor's Note: This new lodging is squeaky clean and in very secluded, scenic location — looks great!

ONTONAGON & SILVER CITY
(PORCUPINE MTNS. & LAKE OF THE CLOUDS)

LAKE OF THE CLOUDS LODGING   (906) 885-5412
CABINS/MOTEL/VACATION HOMES

Only 1 mile from Porcupine Mtn. State Park, on Trail #1, cabins sleep up to 10 and feature fully equipped kitchens, fireplace, TV, VCR, movies. Restaurant within walking distance. The snowmobile trail is 1/2 mile away and alpine and x-country ski areas are two miles away. No pets.

Daily $44-$125

LAKE SHORE CABINS   (906) 885-5318
CABINS

Two miles from the Porcupine Mtns., with 500 ft. frontage on beautiful Lake Superior, experience nature with the calm and comfort of home. Private sandy beach. Fish, hunt, bike, ski, snowmobile, and snowshoe right from your door. All cabins offer housekeeping and include sauna bath and screened porch.

Daily $39-$77 (based on 4 people)

Editor's Note: Well maintained log cabins with a beautiful, large sandy beach!

LAMBERTS CHALET, COTTAGE & VACATION HOMES   (906) 884-4230
RICHARD LAMBERT   CHALETS/HOMES

EDITOR'S ★ CHOICE!

On the sandy shore of Lake superior, these 13 chalets come w/kitchenettes (some w/fireplaces) and 3 vacation homes feature TVs, phone in room, sauna/whirlpool. Enjoy the sandy beaches, grills, picnic tables and Porcupine Mountain; nearby gift shop. Major credit cards. Open all year. Some non-smoking units available. No pets.

Daily   (cottages) $47-$78   (homes) $210-$215

Editor's Note: Very well maintained and comfortable, these small to large homes and chalets will satisfy! See our review this edition.

MOUNTAIN VIEW LODGE   (906) 885-5256 • (800) 435-5256
KIRK   COTTAGES

Contemporary lakeside cottages 1 mile from Porcupine Mtns. Ski hill 2 miles. Snowmobile trail 300 ft. 300 ft. sandy beach. Two bedroom with queen beds, fully equipped kitchen w/dishwasher and microwave. CATV w/videoplayer, fireplace. All lodges w/view of Lake Superior. New 1994. No pets.

Daily $79-$189

MICHIGAN COTTAGES • CHALETS • CONDOS • B&B'S

RAINBOW MOTEL & CHALET

(906) 885-5348
CHALETS/MOTEL

Overlooking Lake Superior and 5 min. from the Porcupine Mtns. large chalets sleep 10 and are furnished (including linens) w/fully equipped kitchens. Some with queen size beds. Enjoy Jacuzzi, sauna, free in-room phone and coffee. New unit with hot tub in room. Restaurant on premises. Credit cards accepted. Open all year. Smoking/pets allowed.

Daily $40-$115 (double occupancy)

Editor's Note: Chalets and motel look very attractive, well maintained and new!

TOIVOLA (TWIN LAKES)

STEVENS RESORT

(906) 288-3719
COTTAGES

Six units, 1-3 bedroom housekeeping cottages on the lake which feature boating, fishing, swimming, and TV. Near golf course, state park, bakery and restaurant. Open year round.

Call for Rates

TWIN LAKES RESORT

(906) 288-3666
COTTAGES

There are 8 units, 2 and 3 bedroom cottages with kitchens, sandy beach, boats and fishing. Located near a golf course and state park. Reservations recommended. Brochure available.

Call for Rates

IRONWOOD & SURROUNDING AREAS

COVERS: BESSEMER • CRYSTAL FALLS • IRON RIVER • LAKE GOGEBIC •
WAKEFIELD • WATERSMEET

Ironwood is known as *"The Big Snow Country"*. But don't let that fool you, it is more than just winter fun. Here among unspoiled forest and mountains are miles of trout streams and hundreds of spring fed lakes. Visitors will enjoy their vacation on the famous Cisco Chain of Lakes, in Bergland/Marenisco. Bring your camera! Here stands "The World's Tallest Indian"—*HIAWATHA*. He towers 150 feet over downtown Ironwood. Also, don't miss the Copper Peak Ski Flying Hill in the Black River Recreation Area, 10 miles northeast of Ironwood.

110

IRONWOOD & SURROUNDING AREAS

(continued...)

Lake Gogebic is the area's largest lake, with 13,000 acres of prime fishing water. In June, September and throughout the season, fishing tournaments are held. Families will enjoy all sorts of summer fun, sightseeing, hiking and water sports. Further northeast we come to the Porcupine Mountains Wilderness State Park (15 miles west of Ontonagon). The Park's 63,000 acres is one of the few remaining large wilderness areas in the midwest and it features the beautiful Lake of the Clouds. Backpacking the "Porkies" is a challenge reserved only for the strong of heart. The Department of Natural Resources maintains over 90 miles of foot trails and more than a dozen rustic trail side cabins.

For additional information regarding events and activities contact:

Gogebic Area Convention & Visitor Bureau
P.O. Box 706
Ironwood, MI 49938-0706
Lodging Referrals: (906) 932-4850
Recreation Reports: (800) 272-7000 (out of Michigan, only)

BESSEMER

BLACKJACK SKI RESORT   (800) 848-1125
CONDOS/CHALETS

Trailside lodging units offer ski-in, ski-out convenience. Cozy fireplaces, new TV systems, complete kitchens, and saunas in every building. Longest run over 1 mile. PSIA Ski School, Kinderkamp and nursery. Units sleep 1, 2, and 3. Special package rates available.

Two Nights $ 65 (and up)
Per Night (prime season) $121 (and up)

BIG POWDERHORN MTN.   (800) 222-3131 • (906) 932-3100
CONDOS/CHALETS

Luxury chalets to budget conscious private chalets and condos provide a wide selection of accommodations. Ice rink, horse-driven sleigh rides, x-country skiing, pool, special events, trailside decks, and live entertainment. NASTAR, ski school, ski shop, rentals, kinderschool, and cafeteria. 3 restaurants and lounges, sauna/whirlpool, and fireplace. Credit cards excepted.

Call for Rates

111

MICHIGAN COTTAGES • CHALETS • CONDOS • B&B'S

HEDGEROW LODGING   **(906) 663-6950**
CHALETS

Ski and snowmobile right out your door! These cozy, clean, comfortable units come with furnished kitchenettes and microwaves. Includes use of pool, sauna and hot tub. Only 5 min. to Indianhead and 10 min. to Big Powderhorn. Special ski packages available!

Call for Rates

CRYSTAL FALLS

BIRCHWOOD CABINS   **(906) 875-3637**
JOHN & SHARON FLOWERS   CABINS

Located on Swan Lake, in a park like setting, these 5 (1 & 2 bedroom) cabins are completely furnished (including linens) and offer utensils, showers and gas heat. Boat included. Excellent hunting/fishing (walleye and perch), plus easy access to hundreds of miles of snowmobile, x-country ski trails. Pets allowed.

Weekly $160-$175

CRYSTAL WATERS RESORT   **(906) 875-6404**
SAM & JOANN PAULSEN   COTTAGES

On Fortune Lake, these 7 ultra-modern, 2-4 bedroom, fully furnished and equipped, lakefront housekeeping cottages (some w/carports) offer gas heat, and color TV. Each has a private dock and use of boat (motor available), sandy beach and diving raft. Fully enclosed fish cleaning house and deep freezer. Great bass, walleye, bluegill, crappie, perch and brook trout fishing.

Call for Rates

TWO-HOUSE-KEY COTTAGES   **(906) UP5-3405**
WALTER & JUNE TUCHOWSKI   COTTAGES

Three cottages (2 and 3 bedrooms) overlook the Fortune Chain of Lakes. Each is completely furnished and equipped (linens/towels provided) with coffee makers, automatic heat, color TV, private dock and use of boat w/ each lodging. They offer a sandy swimming beach and spacious playground area. Excellent fishing, hunting, snowmobiling. Many ski areas nearby. Small pets accepted.

Weekly $300-$325 (up to 4 people — $25 extra per person)

112

IRON RIVER

CATALDO'S CABIN   (906) 265-3991
PHIL & JUNE CATALDO   CHALETS
Two chalet units (3 bedrooms each) on 177 acres of quiet forest land on Stanley Lake. They offer all electric (including heat), 1-1/2 baths. There is abundant wildlife on the property, with plenty of muskie and bass in the Lake. Includes use of boat. 5 min. from Ski Brule Ski Area.

Call for Rates

LAC O'SEASONS RESORT   (906) 265-4881
RANDY & NANCY SCHAUWECKER   COTTAGES
10 min. from downtown Iron River on Stanley Lake, close to groomed x-country ski and snowmobile trails. Facilities feature indoor swimming pool sauna and whirlpool. Newly constructed 2 and 3 bedroom cottages, some log styled, are fully carpeted w/electric heat and appliances. Some units w/fireplaces. Porch w/grills with each unit. Boat, canoe, paddle boats and pontoon rentals.

Call for Rates

PINE WILLOW BED & BREAKFAST   (906) 265-4287
JON & KELLY NELSON   BED & BREAKFAST
Elegant 1926 Colonial Revival home located minutes from recreational activities and ski hill, furnished in a comfortable country style that entices you to relax and enjoy the quiet serenity of 2 wooded acres. There are 8 rooms each with private bath.

Daily $45-$55 sgl. & $45-$75 dbl.

IRONWOOD

BEAR TRACK INN   (906) 932-2144
                                                             CABINS
Located on the western end of Hiawatha National Forest and adjacent to a designated National scenic river. Each cabin is unique and spaced apart from each other. All include complete kitchen, bath, shower, wood burning stoves, and linens. Finnish style wood sauna on premise. Minutes from Lake Superior, waterfalls, hiking/bike trails and more.

Call for Rates

MICHIGAN COTTAGES • CHALETS • CONDOS • B&B'S

BLACK RIVER LODGE   **(800) 666-9916 • (906) 932-3857**
TOWNHOUSES/MOTEL/CONDOS

Located 2 miles from Big Powderhorn Mtn., near Copper Peak Ski Flying Hill
w/7 waterfalls and Black River Harbor. The lodge offers accommodations to fit
all pocketbooks, from motel rooms to spacious townhouses and condominiums.
Indoor swimming pool, restaurant, lounge, and game room.

Call for Rates

LAKE GOGEBIC

THE FISHERMAN RESORT   **(906) 842-3366**
COTTAGES

Well maintained and landscaped grounds on Lake Gogebic. Boats available
for rent—or bring your own! Fully furnished with equipped kitchens, private
baths. Some fireplaces. Bring towels. Cabins sleep 2-8. Gift shop features
handcrafted items. Lodge rooms also available.

Weekly $350 (approx.)

*Editor's Note: Well landscaped resort on the shores of Lake Gogebic. Clean
and comfortable lodgings — great fishing area!*

GOGEBIC LODGE   **(906) 842-3321**
DON/CHRIS/BRIAN BERQUIST   CHALET/MOTEL/COTTAGES

West side of Lake Gogebic, it offers both motel, cottage and chalet
accommodations. Cottages feature private bath, CATV, equipped kitchens,
and more! The Lodge includes sauna/whirlpool, dining room/lounge. Boat
and motor rentals available. Enjoy hunting, fishing, swimming, snowmobiling
and skiing. Credit cards accepted. Pets allowed, extra charge.

Daily $55 (for 2) -$150 (for 6)

*Editor's Note: Their resort has established a good reputation on the lake.
Book reservations early. The three new chalets built in 1994 looked great!*

GRASSO'S WEST SHORE RESORT   **(906) 842-3336**
COTTAGES

450 ft. on Lake Gogebic. Formerly Baily Rustic Resort. Great fishing
for walleye or hunting for bear and deer. All cabins are 2 bedrooms,
sleep 7, bath (towels and linens provided). Boat launch on site, docks
and hoist available. Boat and motor rentals. Pets welcome May-Oct.

Weekly $280 (double occupancy - $25 each additional person)
Daily $50 (double occupancy - $5 each additional person)

*Editor's Note: Small but very clean, comfortable accommodations —
reasonable prices make this one a good choice. See our review this edition.*

114

MALLARD COVE & TEAL WING   **(800) 876-9751**
SNOW COUNTRY ENTERPRISES INC.   **2 PRIVATE VACATION**
TOM & ARLENE SCHNELLER   **HOMES**

Mallard Cove: Spacious 4 bedroom, furnished in Dutch motif and features cedar sauna. Accommodates 10. Features phone, fireplace, Weber grill, full equipped kitchen w/dishwasher, linens, towels. Excellent waterfront view. Boat dock (boat and motor available). Groomed snowmobile trails and skiing nearby.

Teal Wing: Contemporary, spacious home on Lake Gogebic, accented in teal and light oak. 3+ bedrooms (sleeps 8). Fully furnished and equipped including microwaves, phones, TV/VCR's, stereo. Includes use of boat dock (boat and motor available). Also overlooks Lake Gogebic and is located on snowmobile Route #5.

Weekly $800-$900

Editor's Note: The Schneller's have designed and decorated these homes with comfortable elegance. Located on beautiful Lake Gogebic, we highly recommend both Mallard Cove & Teal Wing! See our review in this edition.

NINE PINE RESORT   **(906) 842-3361**
COTTAGES

A family resort, centrally located in "Big Snow Country". Snowmobile right to your door! Modern, carpeted housekeeping units with TV. Restaurants nearby. Open year around. Pets allowed.

Call for Rates

SOUTHWINDS COTTAGE & RUBY SHORES CHALET   **(906) 575-3397**
MARLIN & PAT HANSON   **COTTAGE/CHALETS**

Cottage: Very cozy, clean 2 bedroom cottage on Lake Gogebic with 220 ft. of sandy beach. Private dock. Sleeps 6. All new carpet and furnishings. Fully equipped kitchen with microwave and grill. Private, very quiet. New wood deck overlooking the lake. Rent year around. No pets.

Chalet: Truly the *Gem of Lake Gogebic*. 3100 sq ft. chalet, 4 bedrooms 4 baths, 2 fireplaces, lovely kitchen, dishwasher microwave, hot tub, sauna (w/view of lake), private deck. Docks with 300' of beach. *All brand new*, from chalet to furnishings. Snowmobile, boat and motors, personal watercraft, and bike rentals. No pets.

	Cottage	Chalet
Weekly	$350	$1,250

SUNNYSIDE CABINS   **(906) 842-3371**
SUE GROOMS   **CABINS**

Set along 300 ft. of Lake Gogebic, these 8 well maintained, comfortably furnished lodgings feature fully equipped kitchens including microwaves, knotty pine interiors, satellite TV, private baths, bedrooms with 1 to 2 full size beds. Doorwalls lead to private deck. Linens provided.

Call for Rates

Editor's Note: Spotless cabins with a "luxurious" feel. We were very impressed. See our review in this edition!

MICHIGAN COTTAGES • CHALETS • CONDOS • B&B'S

SUNSET VIEW COTTAGES   **(906) 842-3589**
COTTAGES

New cottages on the East Shore of Lake Gogebic. 2 bedrooms, completely furnished and equipped, knotty pine interiors, cedar exteriors, fully tiled bath/ shower. Accommodates 2-8 people. Individually controlled electric baseboards. Boats available. Great fishing for walleye, bass, and perch. There is a snowmobile trail from your door to the Porcupine Mountains.

Weekly $295-$355   Daily $45-$55 (double occupancy)

THE TIMBER'S RESORT   **(906) 575-3542**
COTTAGES

This year around resort on Lake Gogebic is mid-way between the Porcupine, Indianhead and Powderhorn Mtns. It offers 14 light housekeeping cottages. Enjoy hunting, fishing, snowmobiling, and skiing. Boat and snowmobile rentals available.

Call for Rates

WAKEFIELD

INDIANHEAD BEAR CREEK   **(800) 3-INDIAN**
CONDOS/CHALETS

Facilities offer 2 restaurants, 2 cafeterias, 5 cocktail lounges, indoor pool and spa, health/racquet club, full service ski shop, child care, Kinder Country children's programs (kids 12 and under sleep free w/parents). Enjoy our golfing packages, bicycle tours and races, auto show, kite festival, and more!

Call for Rates

WATERSMEET

ARROW LODGE RESORT   **(906) 358-4390**
COTTAGES/HOMES

Modern/ultra-modern cottages, luxury vacation homes w/fireplaces, TV, dish-washers, whirlpools, microwaves, washers, and dryers. On Thousand Island Lake (Cisco Chain). Up to 15 per home. General store, gift shop, boats, motors, bait, tackle, licenses. Access to snowmobile trails, x-country trails. One hour to downhill skiing.

Weekly $ 330-$1,200

Editor's Note: The interiors of these cottages are well maintained. The newly built cottages were excellent! Beautiful, natural setting — great for fishing and boating.

116

CROOKED LAKE RESORT

(906) 358-4421
COTTAGES

On Crooked Lake, located directly on the water in Sylvania Perimeter/ Wilderness Area. Motors allowed. Easy access to Sylvania x-country ski trails and major snowmobile trails. Six modern (3 new) 2 and 3 bedroom housekeeping cottages. Everything furnished except personal towels. Each cottage has a 14 ft. aluminum boat. Canoe, motor rental, bait, gas also available. Open all year. Pets allowed.

Weekly $375-$575

JAY'S RESORT

(906) 358-4300
COTTAGES

Surrounded by natural woods on Thousand Island Lake. 7 well maintained housekeeping cottages are fully furnished with equipped kitchens and private baths with most facing the water. Sleeps 2-8. Includes boat. Spacious grounds w/ play area, horseshoe pit and picnic area. Bring towels. Call to confirm rates.

Weekly $280-$610

Editor's Note: Cottage exteriors new — the natural grounds were well groomed! Cute play area for children.

LAC LA BELLE RESORT
SKIP & CARYL BUCHANAN

(906) 358-4396
CABINS

These well maintained year around cottages are nestled on Thousand Island Lake and each unit has a view of the water. These heated, 1-2 bedroom units have knotty pine interiors, fully equipped kitchens, linens and blankets are provided (bring your own towels). On the grounds they have a fire pit, fish cleaning station and freezer. Boats, guide service, gas and oil are available.

Weekly $400

Editor's Note: Comfortable and affordable lodgings. Much of the woodworking here has been done by Skip! See our review this edition.

VACATIONLAND RESORT
BILL & JAN SMET

(906) 358-4380
COTTAGES

Housekeeping cottages, 2-6 bedrooms, some w/fireplaces, on Thousand Island Lake. Linens furnished (bring towels). Boat included (motors extra). Safe swimming beach. Dock and raft, tennis, volleyball, basketball, fishing and boating. Great x-country skiing, snowmobiling and ice fishing! Pets allowed.

Call for Rates

REGION 5

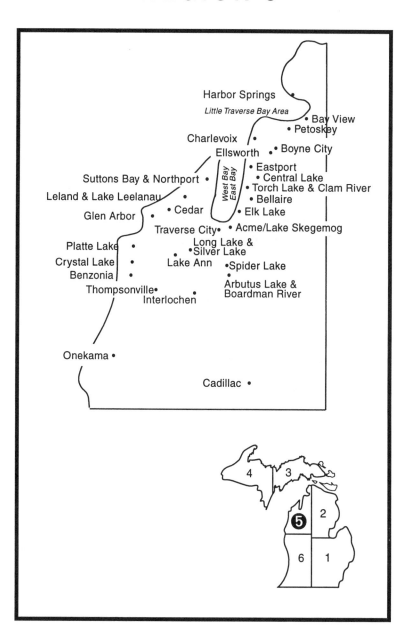

Harbor Springs
Little Traverse Bay Area
• Bay View
• Petoskey
Charlevoix •
Ellsworth • Boyne City
• Eastport
• Central Lake
Suttons Bay & Northport • • Torch Lake & Clam River
West Bay
East Bay
• Bellaire
Leland & Lake Leelanau
• Cedar • Elk Lake
Glen Arbor •
Traverse City • • Acme/Lake Skegemog
Platte Lake •
Long Lake &
• Silver Lake
Crystal Lake • Lake Ann • Spider Lake
Benzonia •
Thompsonville • Arbutus Lake &
Interlochen Boardman River

Onekama •

Cadillac •

4   3
5   2
6   1

REGION 5

There's more to this area than just relaxing on the pure, sandy beaches and watching the sun as it sets on Lake Michigan. It offers miles of scenic drives, wilderness, acres of sand dunes and nature preserves, hundred of lakes, and more varieties of trees than you're likely to find anywhere else! In this area you will also find some of the best salmon, trout and bass fishing in the U.S.A. Within Region 5 lies the Cherry Capital and Summer Golf Capital with many designer golf courses.

If you want things to do, try the festivals, art shows, summer theaters, museums, 19th Century communities and some of the best shopping, gourmet restaurants and winery's around.

The shimmering white now of winter is broken not only by pine trees, deer and elk, but miles of groomed snowmobile trails, cross-country ski trails and some of the Midwest's finest downhill ski runs. Our lake-effect snow is denser, heavier and more durable than mountain snow.

Nature at its most natural, civilization at its most refined.
The perfect blend in any season.

BOYNE CITY • CHARLEVOIX • PETOSKEY

COVERS: BAY VIEW • EASTPORT • ELLSWORTH • HARBOR SPRINGS •
LITTLE TRAVERSE BAY

The scenic area of **Boyne, Charlevoix, Harbor Springs, and Petos key** offers superb sightseeing, unique shops, fishing, sailing, and some of the best downhill and cross country skiing in Lower Michigan! The area also boasts some outstanding restaurants which includes *The Rowe Inn* (Ellsworth), *Tapawingo* (on St. Clair Lake) and *Pete and Mickey's at the Edgewater* (Charlevoix).

Five linear miles of flower-lined streets, a drawbridge, and two lakes have earned **"Charlevoix the Beautiful"** its name. The village has become the center for the arts complete with galleries and shops. The spring offers Petoskey Stone and other fossil collectors, hours of treasure hunting along its many sandy beaches. Don't forget to visit **Petoskey's** unique shops in the historic Gaslight District. **Harbor Springs'** scenic beauty compares to few. Besides its unique shops, take a leisurely drive along the 31 mile route to Cross Villages, through the Tunnel of Trees. Of course, **Boyne's** high peaked hills are, in the wintertime, scene for some of lower Michigan's finest downhill skiing.

Throughout the four seasons, this area has something to offer everyone!

Boyne Country CVB
401 East Mitchell Street
Petoskey, MI 49770
(616) 348-2755 • (800) 456-0197

Charlevoix Area CVB
408 Bridge Street
Charlevoix, MI 49720
(616) 547-2101 • (800) 367-8557

— or call—

The Petoskey-Harbor Springs-Boyne County Visitor's Bureau
(800) 845-2828

BAY VIEW

THE GINGERBREAD HOUSE   (616) 347-3538
MARY GRULER   BED & BREAKFAST

Pastel hues and white wicker provide a romantic setting in this 1881 reno-vated Victorian cottage B&B. Spacious upper suites provide views of Little Traverse Bay. Deluxe home baked continental breakfast. No smoking/pets, please. Open May-October. 5 rooms with private baths.

Daily $60-$110 (dbl)

BOYNE

ATRIUM CONDOS/DILWORTH INN   (800) 748-0160 • (616) 582-6220
MAIN RENTAL OFFICE   CONDOS/INN

Built in 1912 and renovated in 1993, the Dilworth Inn has 26 rooms with A/C. Private baths, suites (multi-rooms), phone and cable TVs in room. Porch surrounds building. Continental breakfast served daily. Excellent dining and lounge with entertainment on weekends. Open year around. Atrium condominium units feature 1-3 bedrooms. Each is fully furnished and offers equipped kitchens (1 bedrooms w/limited kitchens) and fireplaces. Some w/Jacuzzis.

Daily (Inn) $70   Daily (Condos) $80-$140

HARBORAGE CONDOMINIUMS   (800) 456-4313 • (616) 582-3000
MAIN RENTAL OFFICE   CONDOS

2 & 3 bedroom units on the shores of Lake Charlevoix near a full-service marina. Completely equipped and beautifully decorated. Prices exclude holidays.

2 Day Pkg. $375-$400
Weekly $1,275-$1,450

THE LANDINGS   (616) 547-1222
VACATION PROPERTY RENTAL AND MGT. CO.   CONDOS

2 and 3 bedroom condominiums on the shores of Lake Charlevoix in the heart of northwest Michigan's recreational playground! Sandy beach, heated pool, boat slips. Only minutes from Boyne Country Championship Golf. An excellent rental value, located in Boyne City. Call early for best availability.

Weekly $1,200

JOHN C. SCHADE   (313) 675-2452 • (313) 262-3048
                                                                   CONDO

This spacious, 3-level condo overlooks beautiful Lake Charlevoix, is completely furnished (w/linens), and sleeps up to 6. Features king and queen size beds, full kitchen w/microwave, dishwasher, Jenn-Aire grill, 4 baths, fireplace, sauna, private beach and dock, balcony, patio, CATV, washer/dryer. In Boyne City — walking distance to shops. Minimum 1 week rental. $675 non-refundable deposit per week. No pets. References please.

Weekly $ 1,350

WATER STREET INN   **(800) 456-4313 • (616) 582-3000**
MAIN RENTAL OFFICE   CONDOS

On the shores of Lake Charlevoix, these units are set along the sandy beach front near a full-service marina. All 27 bedroom suites have a turn of the century antique decor, Jacuzzi/whirlpool tubs, complete kitchen, gas fireplaces, queen beds. Overnight or weekly packages available. Prices exclude holidays.

	Summer	Other
Daily	$139-$169	$79-$139
Weekly	$989	$589

GREGORY & DIANA YOUNG   **(810) 689-2051**
                                                      VACATION HOME

Near Boyne City (north shore of Lake Charlevoix) this year around lakefront home has 4 bedrooms, 2 baths and is fully furnished (except for linens). Includes washer/dryer, microwave, dishwasher, CATV and sleeps 8. Shared boat docks with 150 ft. of sandy beach. $200 deposit. No pets/smoking.

	July-Aug.	Off Season
Weekly	$925	$375-$775

CHARLEVOIX

AARON'S WINDY HILL GUEST LODGE   **(616) 547-6100 • (616) 547-2804**
                                                      BED AND BREAKFAST

Beautiful Victorian home with a huge riverstone porch where you can relax, visit with friends and enjoy a homemade buffet breakfast. Eight spacious rooms have private bathrooms. Three rooms can accommodate up to five guests. One block north of drawbridge, one block east of Lake Michigan. Open May - Oct.

Daily	$60-$95

GARY & CATHERINE BARNES   **(810) 370-0674(S) • (313) 876-9201(W)**
                                                      CONDO

On Lake Charlevoix, pool, marina, and beach, steps away! Sleep 4 + (bedroom loft and 1st floor bedroom). Deck, skylight, A/C, fireplace, beamed Cathedral ceiling, microwave, 3 CATV, 2 VCRs, CD-cassette, phones, ice maker, laundry. Great for family or 2 couples! No pets.

	Summer	Other
Weekly	$700	$500-$600

MICHIGAN COTTAGES • CHALETS • CONDOS • B&B'S

BOULDER PARK COTTAGES   (810) 626-0460 • (616) 547-6480
JOAN CHODAK   COTTAGES

Stone cottages in Earl Young's Boulder Park — walking distance to town and Lake Michigan. Situated on 2 acres in a private park-like setting. Bed linens, dishwashers, microwaves, CATV and fireplaces. 50% deposit. Pets allowed.

	1 Bedroom	3 bedrooms	
Weekly	$725	$980	(Off-season rates available)

Editor's Note: Part of Charlevoix's history! These cottages are built in the style of Earl Young's boulder homes. Each is uniquely styled.

THE BRIDGE STREET INN   (616) 547-6606
BED & BREAKFAST

Built in 1895, this Colonial Revival home retains all the charm of yesteryear. Relax on its sweeping porch with view of Lake Michigan or in the bright living room. 9 guest rooms attired with old floral rugs on wooden floors, antique furnishings and plush beds. Breakfast and coffee served in the dining room.

Daily $74-$105   (In-season—May to October)

CHARLEVOIX COUNTRY INN   (616) 547-5134
BED & BREAKFAST

Visitors will feel welcomed in this 1896 country decor inn. Relax and get acquainted in the common room, balcony or on the porch while watching boats and colorful sunsets on Lake Michigan. 8 bedrooms and 2 suites (with private bath). Continental breakfast buffet and late afternoon beverage, wine and cheese social.

Daily $50 (upstairs) $125 (downstairs)

SHARON & AL FROST   (616) 536-2851
VACATION HOME

Spacious, 7 bedroom vacation home w/serene setting offers a spectacular view of Lake Charlevoix. Features 3 full baths, large modern kitchen, CATV, fireplace, dock, campfire area, swing set, 3 decks, and 200 ft. of sandy beach. Sleeps up to 25—great for 2 or 3 families! Only 50 ft. from Lake Charlevoix and 5 minutes from town. Great swimming and fishing. Available year around. 50% deposit. No pets.

Weekly (summer) $2,000 (Off-season rates negotiable)

HIDDEN VALLEY RESORT   (616) 547-6244 • (616) 547-1222
JOHN YAROCH   COTTAGES

A destination favorite since 1949, this quiet, unspoiled cottage resort features 620 ft. of natural shoreline on beautiful Nowland Lake, located in the heart of Charlevoix County. Although rustic in atmosphere, each cottage has been cleverly renovated to retain its knotty pine charm, yet provide the modern conveniences of private bath w/shower, fully equipped kitchen, TV,

HIDDEN VALLEY RESORT (...continued)

screened porch, etc. 1 and 2 bedrooms w/sofa sleepers. Sandy beach, excellent fishing lake. 6 miles from Charlevoix, 2 miles from Lake Charlevoix. Linens not provided. Brochure available.

Weekly $350-$500 (Call for availability of 3 and 4 night rentals & rates)

SUE HUMMEL   **(810) 855-3300 • (810) 363-3885**
                                                       CONDOS

Lakefront condos sleep 2 to 12 and offer 1 to 3 baths, A/C, fireplace, 2 person Jacuzzi, and CATV. Designer furnished! Includes linens and laundry. Within walking distance to Charlevoix, marinas, beach. Heated pool. Lots of skiing within 1/2 hour. Available year around. 50% deposit.

Daily (summer)	$75-$125
Weekly (summer)	$400-$1,000

DR. DEBORAH JEAN OR TERRI   **(810) 545-8900**
                                                          COTTAGE

Two log cottages on Lake Michigan, approximately 12 miles from Charlevoix. First sleeps up to 6 and features full kitchen with wood burning stove. Bring your own linens. Second offers 2 bedrooms with loft, sleeps 8, includes washer/dryer and microwave. Near golf, skiing and Michigan's finest gourmet restaurants.

Weekly	Cottage 1 (sleeps 6)	Cottage 2 (sleeps 8)
Sept./Oct.	$350	$600
June-Aug.	$500	$800

LARRY KISH   **(517) 349-5474 HOME • (517) 482-7058 WORK**
                                                    VACATION HOME

Built in 1993, this home features 4 bedrooms/2 baths, 128 ft. water frontage, 600 sq. ft. deck, dock, raft, 5 sliding glass doors and lots of windows. Dishwasher, washer/dryer, TV/VCR and stereo. Vaulted ceiling. Fabulous view. Available year around.

	Sept.-June.	July/Aug.	Xmas/New Years
Weekly	$1,000	$1,500	$2,000

LAKE CHARLEVOIX   **(616) 536-7343**
MARIE YETTAW   COTTAGES

Four, 2 bedroom modern units sleep 2-6. Completely furnished kitchens. Linens included. CATV, picnic table, lawn chairs, barbecue, boat dock, sandy beach. Overlooks the south arm of Lake Charlevoix, 130 ft. of beach. Open all year.

Weekly (summer) $430

MICHIGAN COTTAGES • CHALETS • CONDOS • B&B'S

LAKE CHARLEVOIX HOME
MARIE YETTAW

(616) 536-7343
VACATION HOME

Beautiful 3 bedroom home (sleeps 12) with sandy beach, dock and lawn on Lake Charlevoix. 130' frontage, large decks with BBQ and furniture. Large kitchen, washer, dryer, 6 walkouts, completely furnished, turnkey.

Weekly (summer) $1,740

LAKE CHARLEVOIX - CAPE VICTORIAN
MARIE YETTAW

(616) 536-7343
VACATION HOME

Unique, 2,600 sq. ft., 4 bedroom (sleeps 16), 1890's style Cape Victorian home on 1-1/2 acres with large trees. Quiet setting. Country kitchen, formal dining room, den library, large living room w/wood burning fireplace. 2 full baths. Open all year.

Daily $35 per night/per adult (min. $95)

JOSEPH & BARBARA MARTIN

(313) 625-6248 • (313) 257-5366
COTTAGE

Open year around, modern deck house on Lake Charlevoix. Spectacular sunset view. Completely furnished 3 bedrooms/2 baths, wet bar, wood stove, washer/dryer, complete kitchen includes dishwasher/microwave (linens provided). **Note:** Many steps and decks, may not be suitable for small children (max. 6 people). No pets.

Weekly $1,200-$1,500 (rates seasonal, call to confirm)

POINTES NORTH INN

(616) 547-0055 • (800) 968-5433
CONDOMINIUMS

One and 2 bedroom suites with lofts and full or partial kitchens. Indoor/outdoor pool. CATV, A/C, VCR and Jacuzzi whirlpools in all units. Located in downtown Charlevoix. No pets.

Daily (summer) $150-$ 200

NANCY SERRA

(810) 625-8705
CHALET

In prime golf area. Deck overlooks a panoramic view of Lake Charlevoix. Only steps to beach and conveniently located 2 blocks from marina. Chalet features 3 bedrooms (4 twin, 1 full, 1 queen and queen hide-a-bed). All amenities including CATV and linens. Weekly rentals. $250 deposit. No pets.

Weekly $600

SMUGGLERS' COVE
(616) 536-7343
MARIE YETTAW — CONDOS

These 1 and 2 bedroom units sleep 2-6. Completely furnished with linens, full kitchens, washer and dryer. Includes fireplace, gas grill, patio furniture, CATV, 30 ft. boat wells. Located on the south arm of Lake Charlevoix, sandy beach. Sorry no pets. Open all year.

Weekly $764-$1,275

DUANE TAYLOR
(616) 547-9159
VACATION HOME

Near downtown and beaches (7 blocks to Lake Charlevoix and 5 blocks to Lake Michigan), this lovely 5 bedroom home is fully furnished (linens included) w/large, comfortable deck. Available June 22-Sept. 2. 50% deposit.

Weekly $1,200

UHRICK'S LINCOLN LOG
(616) 547-4881
COTTAGES/MOTEL/CAMPGROUNDS

24 cottages (1, 2 and 3 bedrooms) include full kitchens, CATV and linens. 2 blocks to beach and 1 mile to town. Open April to November. Pets allowed.

Daily $24-$150

VALLEY VIEW RANCH
(616) 348-2765 • (616) 535-2772
VACATION HOME

Overlooks Jordan Valley. Two miles from the south arm of Lake Charlevoix and East Jordan. This home has 3 bedrooms (sleeps 11), 2 baths w/linens. Sofa sleeper in living room, opens before a 22 ft. stone wall w/large fireplace. Cathedral ceiling, piano, microwave, gas grill, deck, TV, VCR, and stereo. Available year around. $200 deposit.

	Summer/Fall	Winter
Weekly	$575	$695

WOODSEDGE
(616) 957-1615 • (616) 582-7626
TOM MOLESTA — VACATION HOME

Spacious lodge w/cathedral ceiling, stone fireplace, abundant kitchen, dining, master room w/sauna and Jacuzzi, 2 guest rooms + loft, laundry room, enclosed porch, lakeside deck w/hot tub. Guest cabin w/fireplace, kitchenette and bath. Limit 10 people. $1,000 deposit. Available year around. No pets/smoking.

Weekly $2,500 (call to verify rates)

EASTPORT

EDEN SHORES   **(616) 547-5316 • (616) 547-5583**
MARILYN & CHARLES WILMOT   **COTTAGE**

Eastport cottage sits in secluded wooded area. Quiet, clean. Bright sunroom with lots of windows. 5 minute walk to Lake Michigan beach. Recently re-done — new carpeting, tile, walls, bathroom. Full kitchen. Linens provided. No pets/smoking.

Weekly $350   Daily (weekends) $100

ELLSWORTH

HOUSE ON THE HILL   **(616) 588-6304**
JULIE & BUSTER ARNIM   **BED & BREAKFAST**

"Our Tenth Season" featured in <u>Detroit Free Press</u>, <u>Chicago Tribune</u>, and <u>Midwest Living</u>. Elegantly furnished Victorian farmhouse. Picture postcard lake views from the veranda. Enjoy a delicious Texas Breakfast and walk to two world class restaurants: **Tapawingo** and **Rowe Inn**. 5 rooms w/private baths.

Daily $85-$115

HARBOR SPRINGS

HAMLET VILLAGE   **(616) 526-2641**
c/o LAND MASTERS   **HOMES & CONDOS**

New, contemporary country styling located in the secluded, rolling hills of Harbor Springs. Slope side condos features ski-in/ski-out access to Nubs Nob. Condos offer 1-3 bedroom + loft. Homes/chalets (between Boyne Highlands and Nubs Nob) vary in size and sleep from 6-12, 1-3 baths. A few miles to beaches/marinas/golf.

	Condos	Homes
Weekly*	$672-$1,834	$546-$1,603 *Call for special package prices

Editor's Note: Great retreat — beautiful setting, lovely interiors. See our review in this edition!

KIMBERLY COUNTRY ESTATE   **(616) 526-7646**
RONN & BILLIE KIMBERLY   **BED & BREAKFAST**

This colonial plantation style B & B welcomes its guests with a lovely veranda and terrace overlooking the swimming pool and Wequetonsing Golf Course. On several secluded acres. Features 6 exquisitely decorated rooms, one w/ wood burning fireplace, sitting area, and four poster bed. 4 min. to Boyne Highlands or Nubs Nobs! 6 rooms.

Daily $135-$225

MAIN STREET BED & BREAKFAST (616) 526-7782
DONNA & JERRY KARSON BED & BREAKFAST

This delightful B&B is as warm and inviting as a Norman Rockwell painting. All guests are treated to a full country breakfast on the wrap around enclosed porch which overlooks the Bay. Conveniently located within walking distance to shops, restaurants, tennis courts, and beaches. 4 rooms.

Daily $70-$90

RATCLIFFE CHALET (313) 852-7833
  CHALET

Spacious 4 bedroom/3 bath chalet sleeps 10 and offers fully equipped kitchen w/microwave, stove, refrigerator, washer/dryer. Three fully furnished levels feature master bedroom w/private dressing room and full bath, ski room, gathering room, bathroom and sauna. Near excellent skiing — Little Traverse Bay.

Call for Rates

TROUT CREEK CONDOMINIUM RESORT (800) 748-0245
  CONDOS

Family oriented condominium resort. Complex includes 3 pools, 2 clubhouses, tennis, grills, hiking trails, near Boyne Highlands. Special golf/tennis packages available. Minutes from beaches.

Daily $70-$110   Weekly $780-$1,200

Editor's Note: Contemporary setting with plenty to do for couples or families. See our review in this edition!

LITTLE TRAVERSE BAY

HOLIDAY ACCOMMODATIONS (800) 968-4353 • (616) 348-2765
TONI MATTHEWS CONDOS/CHALETS/COTTAGES

A variety of cottages, chalets and condos are offers throughout the Little Traverse Bay area. From 1 bedroom log styled chalet to 4 bedroom homes and condos. Prices to fit all budgets.

Weekly $425-$1,325

PETOSKEY (WALLOON LAKE)

BEAR RIVER VALLEY BED & BREAKFAST (616) 348-2046
RUSS & SANDRA BARKMAN BED & BREAKFAST

A north woods retreat in the heart of northern lower Michigan. Comfort and luxury in a spectacular, sylvan setting. Close to lakes, beaches, shops, galleries, gourmet restaurants, ski hills, and trails. Three rooms share 2 baths. Authentic Finnish sauna, healthy Gourmet Continental Breakfast. No smoking. No pets.

Daily $60-$75

MICHIGAN COTTAGES • CHALETS • CONDOS • B&B'S

BENSON HOUSE BED & BREAKFAST   **(616) 347-1338**
ROD & CAROL BENSON   **BED & BREAKFAST**

1878 Victorian, formerly the Ozark Hotel. Located 3 blocks from Petoskey's famed Gaslight Shopping District. Large rooms, private baths; 80' veranda overlooks Little Traverse Bay. Full breakfast — wine and snacks in afternoon. Close to golf, beaches, boating, downhill and x-country skiing. No pets/smoking.

Daily $78-$112

BARBARA MOYERS   **(313) 668-8507 (W) • (616) 347-4043 (S)**
COTTAGE

Spacious, multi-level cottage on the west side of Walloon Lake. 4 bedrooms, 2 full baths, 2 kitchens, plus extra sleeping area (can sleep 10). Fully furnished, wood burning cast iron fireplace, electric heat. Bring your own linens. Includes 15 ft. aluminum boat. Also features lounge deck and fire pit. Great fishing! Prefer 2 weeks rental but will except 1 week. No pets/smoking please.

	May, June - Aug.	Winter
Weekly	$575-$1,265	$750

TRAVERSE CITY & SURROUNDING AREAS

COVERS:
ACME • ARBUTUS LAKE • BELLAIRE • BENZONIA • BORDMAN RIVER • CEDAR • CENTRAL LAKE • CLAM LAKE • CRYSTAL LAKE • EAST BAY • ELK LAKE • GLEN ARBOR • GRAND TRAVERSE BAY • INTERLOCHEN • LAKE ANN • LAKE LEELANAU • LAKE SKEGEMOG • LELAND • LONG LAKE • NORTHPORT • PLATTE LAKE • SCHUSS MOUNTAIN • SILVER LAKE • SPIDER LAKE • SUTTONS BAY • THOMPSONVILLE • TORCH LAKE • WEST BAY

From beautiful sunsets and lazy days on a sandy beach to the rush of downhill skiing—**Traverse City** and the surrounding areas have a variety of fun and excitement in a setting of blue waters, rolling hills, and natural beauty! Dining, shopping, entertainment, and even gambling will fill your days and nights.

Just a few of the many excellent restaurants include: *Hattie's Grill* or *Boone's Prime Time Pub* (Sutton's Bay), *The Trillium, Papparazzi* or *Orchard Room* (Grand Traverse Resort), *Boone's Long Lake Inn, The Embers, Sweitzer's by the Bay* (Traverse City), or *Scott's Harbor Grill* (M-22 on Sleeping Bear Bay beach), *Windows* (on M-22, N. of Traverse City), *LeBear* (M-22 in Glen Arbor).

TRAVERSE CITY & SURROUNDING AREA

(continued...)

Take a ride on the Malabar, a two-masted schooner, or tour the Bay in a hot air balloon. Be sure to visit the Big Red Barn Music House north of Traverse. Your trip to this area would not be complete unless you visit the many wineries and sample some of Michigan's finest made wines.

For additional information regarding events and activities in the area contact:

Grand Traverse CVB
415 Munson Avenue, Suite 200
Traverse City, MI 49684
(800) 872-8377

ACME

GRAND TRAVERSE RESORT   **(800) 748-0303 • (616) 938-2100**
                                                                        CONDOS

Luxury condos — some w/wet bars, whirlpool baths, and fireplaces. Grand Traverse offers casual to fine dining in its 10 restaurants and lounges. Also featured are shopping galleries, indoor-outdoor tennis, weight room, indoor-outdoor pools, and aerobic studio. Well groomed x-country ski trails and 36 holes of championship golf including *"The Bear"*.

Call for Rates

ARBUTUS LAKE

GEORGE CZANSTKE   **(810) 373-0005 • (616) 947-0039**
                                                                VACATION HOME

Situated on Arbutus Lake with 200 ft. of private sandy beach, this 5 room, 2 bedroom and 1 bath, log cottage is furnished w/fireplace and a fully equipped kitchen. It also offers dock, pontoon boat and raft. Sleeps 5. No pets.

Weekly $700

MAC'S LANDING RESORT   **(616) 947-6895**
                                                                        COTTAGES

14 cottages (1-3 bedrooms, sleeps 2-8) on 700 ft. of beautiful lakefront property offers a scenic setting and sandy beach. Features docks, great swimming, raft, boats and motors, campfire pits, playground, volleyball, and horseshoes. Bring linens. Open June-Sept. Pets allowed.

Weekly $250-$600

131

MICHIGAN COTTAGES • CHALETS • CONDOS • B&B'S

PINEVIEW RESORT   **(616) 947-6792**
                                              COTTAGES/APTS.
12 cottages and apartments are on the lake (some w/fireplaces). Fire pit on beach, lounge deck and dock on lake. Enjoy volleyball, shuffleboard, horseshoes, and playground area. Boats, motors, pedal boats, and pontoons available for rental. 2-3 bedrooms (sleeps 5-8). $125 deposit required.

Weekly $440-$520

SHADYCREST RESORT   **(616) 947-9855**
                                              COTTAGES
These 9 cottages (some w/fireplaces) have 1 and 2 bedrooms and sleep 4-8. Includes use of boat. Boat motors are available for rent. Open April-Nov. Pets allowed.

Weekly * $275-$425
* Rates based on 2 adults w/children. Reduced rates Sept.-May

BELLAIRE

GRAND VICTORIAN B&B INN   **(800) 336-3860 • (616) 533-6111**
JILL & GEORGE WATSON   BED & BREAKFAST
1895 Victorian mansion built by lumber barons. On National Register. Inn features antiques, 3 fireplaces, etched glass and wicker-filled porch/balconies overlooking park. Gourmet breakfast. 4 rooms w/private baths. No smoking.

Daily $65-$95

GRASS RIVER BED & BREAKFAST   **(616) 533-6041**
HARRIETT BEACH   BED & BREAKFAST
Modern comfort in a secluded location 2.5 miles from Bellaire on Grass River. Hiking, biking, x-country ski trails. Dock for boat, fishing, swimming and tubing. Hot tub and sun room adjacent to natural area. Full breakfast, 3 rooms w/private baths. Open May 1-Oct. 31

Daily $65-$85

MAPLES RESORT   **(616) 533-8293**
GREG   COTTAGES
Two miles from Bellaire on the Chain of Lakes, these 9 cottages (fully re-modeled in 1990) are nestled in 8 acres of heavily wooded and landscaped grounds. 1,2 & 3 bedroom units offer lake views and include use of grill, boat and launch. Sailboats, pontoons, motors available. Excellent swimming beach! Bonfires every night. No pets.

Weekly $425-$530

132

SHANTY CREEK RESORT   **(800) 678-4111 • (616) 533-8621**
ROOMS/CHALETS/CONDOS

Four season resort on the lake. 3 championship golf courses including "The Legend" by Arnold Palmer. 29 downhill ski slopes, 31 km of x-country trails, ski school. Other amenities include tennis, mountain biking, health club, hiking, beach club and indoor/outdoor pools. Fine dining, live entertainment. 600 rooms, condos and chalets some with full to partial kitchens, fireplaces, Jacuzzis. Great swimming. No pets.

Weekly   Begins at $625 (per person based on double occupancy)

BENZONIA

HANMER'S RIVERSIDE RESORT   **(800) 252-4286 RESERV. • (616) 882-7783**
JOHN & BARBARA HANMER   COTTAGES

On the Betsie River, located at the Gateway of the Sleeping Bear Dunes National Lakeshore. New two bedroom housekeeping units are completely furnished with equipped kitchens, A/C, CATV, phone. Decks overlook the river. Enjoy the new pool and Jacuzzi! Open year around. Summer fun, winter skiing and snowmobiling, fall/spring steelhead/salmon fishing. No pets.

Weekly $259-$427   Daily $40-$65

BOARDMAN RIVER

SUE, KELLY & ROBERT SCHMELTZER   **(810) 478-7247**
COTTAGE

Private 4 room, 2 bedroom cottage (sleeps 6). Nestled in 10 acres of woods by the Boardman River. Includes fully equipped kitchen, spa bath, BBQ, patio, hot tub, fireplace, A/C and VCR. Enjoy tubing, horseback riding, canoeing, and dining. Only 3-1/2 miles from Ranch Rudolf. Approx. 14 miles to Traverse City. No pets.

Weekly $950

CEDAR

SUGAR LOAF RESORT   **(616) 228-7093**
MIKE   **CHALET/TOWNHOUSE**
Amenities include golfing, Lake Michigan beach, 3 swimming pools, tennis, casino, biking and hiking.

Weekly   From $350

CENTRAL LAKE

BOB & BETTY KACZMAREK   **(810) 363-8814**
     COTTAGES
Three cottages all w/2 bedrooms (sleeps 6). Fully furnished. Kitchens with refrigerators, stoves, microwaves, cooking and eating utensils, TVs and VCRs, gas grills, fire pit, picnic table and patio furniture. Includes use of pontoon and fishing boat. Properties include:

River's Edge—Attractive, modern cottage on Hanley Lake. Features bath/tub shower, screened porch. Short walk to town, beach, park.

Weekly $450   Weekend $250

Editor's Note: Quiet setting with a delightful view of the river from the cheery screened porch make River's Edge a delight.

Lakeside & Sleepy Hollow— 2 attractive, modern cottages on Hanley Lake. Features private bath with shower stall and screened porch. Short distance to town, beach and park.

Weekly $400   Weekend $225

CLAM LAKE

NORTHAIRE RESORT   **(616) 347-1250**
MIKE & HELEN LAMBERT   **COTTAGES**
6 cottages, completely furnished except linens and towels. 340 ft. frontage on Clam Lake in 60 + mile Chain of Lakes. Great fishing! Golf, shopping, restaurants close by. Docks, rowboats, paddle boat, screened porches, grills, picnic tables. Cable-ready for your TV. Serene setting, sandy bottom, near nature preserve and marina. Open April 1 to Nov. 1. Pets O.K.!

	2 Bedroom	3 Bedroom
Weekly	$395	$455-$595
Daily	$50	$60-$66

CRYSTAL LAKE

BRUCE (313) 642-9595
COTTAGE

This waterfront 2 bedroom family cottage sleeps up to 6 (first bedroom w/ double bed, second bedroom with 4 single, built-in beds). Set on the north shore of Crystal Lake, it is 30 miles west of Traverse City. Located 15 ft. from the water, its private beach and dock has excellent swimming with a very gradual, sandy beach! Fish for perch and lake trout while you're here!

Call for Rates

EAST BAY

BAYSIDE RESORT (616) 943-4128
TOM BRADY COTTAGES & HOME

Three private cottages (2 or 4 bedroom) each with 100 ft. lake frontage. Well decorated, fully furnished and equipped. Includes microwaves, dishwashers, washers/dryers, cable TV, grill, dock and use of fishing boat. Larger home also features whirlpool with view of bay from all rooms. Linens provided. No pets.

	July/Aug.	June/Sept./Oct.
Weekly	$600-$1,650	$300-$850

THE BEACH CONDOMINIUMS (616) 938-2228
CONDOS

These 30 luxury condos on Grand Traverse Bay feature private sun decks (sleeps 4), whirlpool baths, complete kitchen and 27" stereo CATV. Beautiful sandy beach, outdoor heated pool and hot tub, and daily housekeeping. Adjacent boat launch and close to championship golf. AAA discount, daily rentals, getaway and ski packages.

Call for Rates

TOM & CYNTHIA LATTIN (313) 455-8711
HOME

Privately owned 2 level home on large lot with 100 ft. of sandy beach. Three bedrooms, 2 baths, full kitchen/dining area and family/living room. Upper level overlooks East Bay. Completely furnished (bring your own linens), picnic table, grill, lawn furniture, CATV, and microwave. No pets.

	June/Sept.	July/Aug.
Weekly	$350	$800

MICHIGAN COTTAGES • CHALETS • CONDOS • B&B'S

NORTH SHORE INN   **(800) 968-2365 • (616) 938-2365**
                                                              CONDOS

Set on 200 ft. of private sandy beach on East Bay, these 26 luxury condos
offer 1 & 2 bedrooms. Spectacular views of bay from front decks and
balconies. Outdoor pool, sun deck. Full-size kitchens, dishwashers,
microwaves, queen-size beds, remote TV w/HBO, VCR. Special fall, winter
and spring weekend packages. Open year around.

Call for Rates

OLD MISSION INN   **(616) 223-7770**
                                           COTTAGES/APTS./LOG CABIN

These 7 cottages and 2 apartments are located on Old Mission Rd. Lodgings
range in size from 1-5 bedrooms, and sleep 4-10 (some w/fireplaces). Handicap
access available. Log home also available and includes 6 rooms (3 bedrooms),
sleeps 7. Boat extra.

Weekly $250-$400 (log home weekly rental $500)

ON A BAY RESORT   **(616) 938-2680**
STEVE/PAT AVERY   **COTTAGES**

These 21 units offer from 1-3 double beds. Some w/refrigerator and microwave.
Most have complete kitchens. All bedding furnished. Clean towels supplied daily
upon request. This resort offers CATV and beautiful sundeck.

Call for Rates

STONEWALL INN   **(616) 223-7800**
                                                             COTTAGE

Privately owned log cottage built in 1986 situated on Old Mission Harbor.
Has fully equipped kitchen, fireplace, 2 full baths, private beach, washer/
dryer, porch overlooking the water. No pets.

Weekly $700   (May-Nov. 1st)

SUGAR BEACH RESORT   **(616) 938-2160**
BETTY & ROGER BOGIN   **COTTAGES**

Located on the "Miracle Mile" w/110 ft. of sugar sand beach, this resort offers
9 cottages (studio & 2 bedroom). All include kitchenettes, complete bedding,
and clean towels. Plus, CATV, BBQ's, picnic tables, play area, and lounge
chairs. Open year around. $150 deposit. No pets.

Weekly $650-$800

WINTERWOOD ON THE BAY   **(616) 929-1009**
R. SCHERMERHORN   **COTTAGE**

Recently built beach house, located on East Bay. Sleeps 4 (2 bedrooms), bath,
kitchen, living/dining room, fireplace, hot tub on outside deck. Dishwasher,
microwave, VCR and cable TV. Fully furnished kitchen. Linens provided.
Private dock. No pets.

Weekly $725

136

ELK LAKE

CEDARS END ON ELK LAKE
DEAN & SHARON GINTHER

(214) 424-2858 • (616) 322-6286
VACATION HOME

Spacious 3 bedroom, 2 bath home on 450 ft. of private east Elk Lake frontage. Furnished, dishwasher, microwave, cookware, 2 fireplaces, dock with boat mooring. 50 acres of woodland attached. Excellent swimming, hiking, boating and fishing. No linens. No pets. Available July-October.

Weekly $1,100 (off season $700)

KEWADIN LAKESHORE LODGE

(616) 264-8340
COTTAGES/EFFICIENCIES/MOTEL

With Elk Lake frontage, this resort offers cottages, efficiencies and motel type accommodations. Four units offer full kitchens and color TV. Boats, picnic tables and gas grills included. Paddle boats and two docks available to guests. Recreation room features pool table, ping pong and more. No pets.

Call for Rates

THE PINES COTTAGES

(616) 267-5263
COTTAGES

10 log cottages w/fireplace on 230 ft. of Elk Lake. Features 1-3 bedrooms, partial kitchens, playground area, dock and swimming beach. Open year around. Daily rates available. No pets.

Weekly $275-$525

WANDAWOOD RESORT & RETREAT CENTER

(616) 264-8122
COTTAGES/DUPLEXES

On Elk Lake, 13 cottages with lakefront and orchard settings. Each varies in size from small 1 bedroom cottage to duplex units and a large 5 bedroom home. Full kitchen and bath facilities. Features 9 beach areas, each with docks, plus 2 swimming rafts. Rowboats, canoes and paddle boards available. Open area for field sports and a paperback book library for those quiet times.

Weekly $310-$965

MICHIGAN COTTAGES • CHALETS • CONDOS • B&B'S

WHISPERING PINES
JERRY MCKIMMY

(616) 264-5424
LAKEFRONT HOME

3 bedroom ranch w/walkout lower level on the west side of Elk Lake (100 ft). Summer rental, max. 10 people. Fully furnished and equipped with central air, washer/dryer, microwave, dishwasher, cable TV and VCR. Linens provided. Excellent sandy beach. Bonfires allowed. Grill, volleyball, ping pong. No smoking/pets, please.

Weekly $1,400

WHITE BIRCH LODGE

(616) 264-8271 • (616) 264-5823
RESORT

This American Plan Resort (3 meals included in price) offers a variety of accommodations — from lodge rooms to deluxe townhouse apartments and a whole lot of summer fun activities. On Elk Lake there's plenty of swimming, sailing, wind surfing, water skiing and fishing.

Call for Rates

GLEN ARBOR

ELK RAPIDS BEACH RESORT

(800) 748-0049
CONDOS

Luxury condos overlooking Grand Traverse Bay, just minutes from Traverse City. Heated pool, in room Jacuzzi and full size kitchen.

Daily $189 (for 2 nights)

THE HOMESTEAD
MAIN OFFICE RENTALS

(616) 334-5000
CONDOS

One mile of frontage on Lake Michigan, 3 miles on Crystal River, surrounded by the Sleeping Bear Dunes. This secluded resort offers shops, golf academy, tennis, pools, restaurants, x-country and downhill skiing, conference centers, lodge rooms, suites and condos ranging from studio to 4 bedrooms. Closed late Oct. through Christmas and mid-March through May (open winter weekends).

Weekends* $145-$466   Weekly* $825-$3,260
*Please contact rental office for special package prices.

138

WHITE GULL INN   **(616) 334-4486**
S. W. THOMPSON   **BED & BREAKFAST**
Older 2 story home on a lovely wooded lot in the village of Glen Arbor. Nestled between Sleeping Bear Sand Dunes and the lake shore of Sleeping Bear Bay. Walking distance to shops, restaurants, tennis courts, hiking trails. Short drive to golf courses and Glen Lakes. Come enjoy the friendly atmosphere of White Gull Inn's 5 rooms. Major credit cards accepted.

Daily $61

GRAND TRAVERSE BAY

ROGER & PHYLLIS BROWNE   **(517) 792-8290**
                                      VACATION HOME
Built in 1989, this luxury home features 7 bedrooms (sleeps 14), 4 full and 2 half baths, wrap around deck, 150 ft. of sandy beach on Lake Michigan. Indoor swimming pool, Jacuzzi, sauna, washer, dryer, dishwasher, 2 ovens, microwave/convection, TV/VCR. No smoking. No pets.

Weekly $3,800

TRAVERSE BEACH MOTEL • CONDO   **(800) 634-6113 • (616) 946-5262**
                                         MOTEL/CONDO
This all season resort is located on 700 ft. of sugar sand beach on the East Arm of Grand Traverse Bay. All units face the water and include double or queen size beds and refrigerator. Some include kitchen, microwave, whirlpool tubs, wetbar, and /or patios/balconies. Sleeps 2-6 people.

Daily $48-$198

INTERLOCHEN

BROOKSIDE COTTAGES   **(616) 276-9581**
JOE & NANCY MAREK   **COTTAGES**
Located in the Traverse City/Interlochen area, with 250 ft. lake frontage, these 13 cottages vary in size (studio - 3 bedrooms) and sleeps 6. Includes fully equipped kitchens. Motor rentals available. $150 deposit required. Open year around. No pets.

Weekly* $315-$500 * Off-season rates available

MICHIGAN COTTAGES • CHALETS • CONDOS • B&B'S

ELLIS LAKE RESORT   (616) 276-9502
CABINS

Cozy 1 room cabins on the lake, surrounded by forest. Retreat-like atmosphere. Price includes outdoor hot tub, boats, canoes, linen service and much more. Open year around. Resort was featured in *Midwest Living Magazine* and enjoys an 80% customer return and referral rate. Pets allowed.

Weekly $395-$495

MARY MUELLER & MARK PAYNE   (616) 276-6756
CABIN

Cozy cabin on 1-1/2 wooded acres with 125' Green Lake frontage. One bedroom with additional set of bunk beds. Sleeps 2-4. Fully equipped kitchen with microwave. Provide your own linens/towels. Large wood deck. Private dock and 10' rowboat included. Open May-Sept. Non-smoking. Pets allowed.

Weekly $295

LAKE ANN

BIRCH GLEN RESORT   (616) 275-7340
VIRGINIA CULLEN   **CABINS**

Open year around. All cabins include screened porch and fishing boat. Sandy beach, fire pit, kids playhouse on premises. Motor rentals available, bait sold. Two bedroom cabins sleep 4. Three bedroom cabins sleep 8.

Weekly* $375-$475   *Nightly and off-season rates available

LAKE LEELANAU

GREAT ESCAPE RESORT   (810) 375-0425
MARK & RENEE SMITH   **VACATION HOME**

Three bedroom home (sleeps 8), 2 full baths — great sunsets. Redwood deck overlooks trees/lawn and leads to beach. Home features fireplace, attached garage, microwave, CATV, stereo, grill, and more! 10 min. from Traverse City & 15 min. from Sugar Loaf. Open year around. No pets.

Weekly $1,200 (Off-season $650)

JOLLI LODGE   (616) 256-9291
Cottages/Apts./Lodge

This homey retreat offers a great view of Lake Michigan from their 5 cottages, 11 apartments and 6 lodge rooms. Apartments (1-3 bedrooms) are newer.

140

JOLLI LODGE (CONTINUED...)
Cottages and lodge simply furnished but clean. Several steps down leads to pebbled beach. Tennis, rowboat, kayaking, volleyball and shuffleboard. Open May-Oct.

Weekly $480-$800   Daily $70-$75

MARLENE VANVOORST   **(616) 941-1663 • (616) 256-7602**
                                                          VACATION HOME
Lakefront home, on east shore, 2 bedrooms plus loft (can sleep 6). Screened porch. Furnished except linens. Includes use of rowboat. Safe swimming. No pets.

Weekly $465 (and up)

WEST WIND RESORT   **(616) 946-9457**
                                                COTTAGES
Ten cottages feature 2 to 4 bedrooms (sleeps 4-8) some w/fireplaces. Facilities have children's playground, hot tubs, paddle boards, pedal boats, and protected harbor. No pets.

Weekly $650-$1,300

LAKE SKEGEMOG

JOHN KING   **(313) 349-4716**
                              HOME
Lakefront home on 100 ft. of sandy beach near Traverse City. 4 bedrooms, 2 baths, fully furnished with fireplace. Spacious deck overlooking Lake Skegemog which is part of Elk-Torch chain of 5 lakes. Rowboat. Very clean. One family limit. No smoking/pets.

Weekly $900

LELAND

MANITOU MANOR   **(616) 256-7712**
                                        BED & BREAKFAST
Beautifully restored 1900 farmhouse surrounded by cherry orchards and woods. Queen size beds, private baths, on the main floor in the wing of the home. Huge parlor with fieldstone fireplace and TV. Breakfast features **Leelanau County** specialties. Near sand dunes, bike trails, beaches, golf, x-country and downhill skiing. Non-smoking. No pets. Open all years. 4 rooms.

Daily $75-$110

LONG LAKE

BRICK'S COTTAGE   **(616) 946-1697**
BOB & NANCY BRICK   COTTAGE

A 4 bedroom (sleeps 7) home offering hardwood floors, oak paneling, open living area w/fireplace. Beautiful setting with great views, excellent fishing and recreation, with sandy lake bottom. Fully furnished (except linens). Includes use of fishing boat and dock. Available year around. No pets/smoking.

Weekly $850 (Off-season rates available)

STEVE & STEPHANIE GENTILE   **(513) 871-2435**
                                                                 COTTAGE

Newer three bedroom lake front home in quiet setting, incredible sunsets. Decking tiered to private dock. Shallow, sandy swimming, rowboat. Open living/dining area, fireplace, floor to ceiling windows. Kitchen equipped with dishwasher, microwave, cable TV and telephones. Rowboat included. Six miles to Traverse City, 4 miles to Interlochen. Bring linens. No pets/smoking.

Weekly $900

RON JONES OR FRED JONES   **(616) 946-5119**
                                                                 COTTAGE

Two bedroom log cottage w/knotty pine interior features fireplace (wood provided), color TV and full kitchen with microwave. Private beach, dock, 12' aluminum boat, gas BBQ grill, picnic table, lawn furniture. Bring linens. Located 6 miles from Traverse City. Available year around. Pets allowed.

Weekly $525

NORTHPORT

BIRCH BROOK   **(616) 386-5188**
LYN & GEORGE ANDERSON   **BED & BREAKFAST**

A charming colonial style home set on two well-groomed acres surrounded by a sparkling brook. Decorated with lovely antiques. Eat an extended continental breakfast in the dining room or in the adjoining greenhouse. Guided x-country skiing during winter. 3 rooms (shared and private baths). No pets/smoking.

Daily $50-$65 ($65 Private bath)

142

NORTH SHORE INN   **(616) 386-7111**
SUSAN HAMMERSLEY   **BED & BREAKFAST**
A great sunrise over Grand Traverse Bay from luxurious waterfront rooms in this elegant, spacious home built in 1946 in the colonial tradition. Private baths, fireplaces, sandy beach, porches and decks. Join your hosts for afternoon appetizers and a gourmet breakfast. Excellent golf and x-country skiing nearby. Closed March & April. 4 rooms.

Daily $125   (Each additional guest $25)

PLATTE LAKE AREA

BEAUTIFUL DUNES EDGE HOME   **(313) 676-2497**
MARK & CATHY HUGHES   **LAKEFRONT HOME**
Large home located on 140 ft. of private lake frontage that is surrounded by Sleeping Bear Dunes. Features 4 large bedrooms, 2 full baths, fireplace, deck, nature and x-country ski trails. Fully equipped kitchen. Private deck with 12 ft. rowboat and paddle boat. Available year around. No pets.

Weekly $1,100   (Daily rates in winter $170)

PLATTE LAKE RESORT I   **(616) 325-6723**
    COTTAGES
On beautiful Big Platte Lake. These 1, 2 & 3 bedroom cottages are completely furnished and carpeted with kitchenettes. All include linens, dishes, cable TV, picnic tables and grills. Fishermen and hunters welcome. Open April-November. Daily and weekly rentals. No pets.

Daily $40 and up (based on number of people)

RIVERSIDE   **(616) 325-2121**
    COTTAGE
All season fun! Fish, swim, canoe, hike, snowmobile, ski, sightsee...be "Up North". Newer home, built in 1990, located on The Platte River in Honor, MI. 4 bedrooms, 2 baths, fully equipped kitchen, cable TV. Provide own linens. No pets. Available year around.

Weekly $300   Daily $65

SCHUSS MOUNTAIN

RICHARD & JO-ANN SOCHA
(313) 663-3766
CHALET

This 3 bedroom, 2 bath, year around chalet sleeps 8 and offers a secluded setting. Completely furnished w/fireplace (wood provided), dishes, linens and maid service. It sets at the top of Schuss Mt. and offers ski-in, ski-out. A mecca for golfers, swimming pools in village. No pets/smoking.

Weekly $600   Daily $180

CLARE TAYLOR
(517) 394-4162
CONDOMINIUM & CHALET

Two privately owned properties are available for daily or weekly rental:

Condo: New 2 bedroom/1 bath condo is located on the 1st fairway of Schuss Mountain's golf course. Features deck, telephone, A/C, CATV, fireplace fully equipped kitchen w/microwave and dishwasher. Linens provided. Use of hot tub, pool and sauna at Schuss Lodge. Available year around. No pets.

Weekly $350-$500   Daily $100-$180

Chalet: Located on a secluded lot in the wooded, rolling hills area of Schuss Mountain has 3 bedrooms/2 baths. Lodging features a fully equipped kitchen w/microwave, ski storage area, electric heat, CATV w/remote control, and telephone. Linens provided. Use of hot tub, pool and sauna at Schuss Lodge. Available year around. No pets.

Weekly $350-$500   Daily $100-$180

SILVER LAKE

TOM BRADY
(616) 943-4128
COTTAGES

Two private cottages, each with 2 bedrooms, with 100 ft. of lake frontage. All lodgings well decorated, fully furnished and equipped with microwave, dishwasher, cable TV and deck. Dock and use of fishing boat included. Newer cottage features two baths and fireplace. Linens provided. No pets.

	July/Aug.	June/Sept./Oct.
Weekly	$600-$700	$300-$350

144

GERALD NIEZGODA **(616) 943-9630**
COTTAGE

Furnished vacation cottage on Silver Lake offers 80 ft. private frontage, 2 bedrooms (sleeps 4-6), sandy beach, swimming, fishing, sailing, skiing, outstanding view. Only 2 miles from new mall and 4 miles to Traverse City. Includes CATV, microwave, boat and dock. Bring towels. Open all year around. No pets/smoking.

Weekly $525   (Based on occupancy of 4)

RAYMOND PADDOCK & JILL HINDS **(616) 943-8506**
COTTAGE

Fully furnished 3 bedroom cottage accommodates 8 people and features full kitchen, fireplace, stereo, TV, grill, and 2 decks. Also features dock, swim raft, canoe and rowboat. Open June-Sept.

Weekly $500

SPIDER LAKE

TOM & JANET BABEL **(616) 941-1298**
VACATION HOME

Recently remodeled waterfront cottage on Spider Lake (90 ft. frontage). Fully furnished with 2 bedrooms (sleeps 6), 1 bath. Includes dock, canoe, beach, picnic area. Excellent fishing. Approx. 15 minutes from Grand Traverse Bay and downtown. Rent June-August. No pets.

Weekly $700   Monthly $2,200

BEACH HOUSE @ SPIDER LAKE **(616) 946-5219**
ROLF & KATHY SCHLIESS COTTAGE

Lots of fun & sun! This 2 bedroom, 1 bath home also includes a bunk house, large family room with a huge brick fireplace, full kitchen with microwave, sandy beach and dock. Boat included — motor available. Available year around. Pets allowed.

Weekly (summer) $800-$850

HAROLD'S RESORT **(616) 946-5219**
ROLF & KATHY SCHLIESS COTTAGES

Seven log-style cabins sit on a private peninsula by Spider Lake and offer a terrific sandy beach. Open year around. Weekends, romance, bed & breakfast package rates available. Each feature wonderful views, kitchens, carpet. No pets.

Weekly (summer) $295/2 people and $420-$495/4 people

MICHIGAN COTTAGES • CHALETS • CONDOS • B&B'S

L' DA RU LAKESIDE RESORT, INC.   **(616) 946-8999**
DANNY & JILL RYE   COTTAGES

With 455' lake frontage, this lodge, built in 1923, was once the hideout
for Al Capone. Come see how the notorious lived. The 17 cottages,
added in the mid-1950's, have all been updated. Each is complete
with eating and cooking utensils, coffee maker and toaster + 20"
CATVs. Linens and bedding are provided. Boats included — motors
available. Good swimming beach! Towels are $8 per person for a
week. Open year around. No pets.

	Summer	Off Season
Weekly	$445-$880	$650
Daily	n/a	$50-$130

JACK & ROSEMARY MILLER   **(616) 947-6352**
                                          COTTAGE

Attractive lakefront log cottage on Spider Lake. Offers knotty pine interior, 2
bedrooms (w/linens), fireplace, electric heat, TV and complete kitchen
including microwave. This quiet, quaint hide-away is furnished with antiques,
oak dining set, china cabinet, brass bed, and marble top dresser. 13 miles
from Traverse City. No pets.

Weekly $365   (May-Oct.)

MOONLIGHT BAY RESORT   **(616) 946-5967**
ROGER & NANCY HENDRICKSON   COTTAGES

Beautiful wooded setting surrounds our private 8 cottage resort, with direct
frontage on Spider Lake. Our 1, 2 and 3 bedroom cottages are modern
and fully furnished. Rowboats, canoes, pedal boat included. Motor and
pontoon boat rental available. Open year around. No pets please. For free
brochure call or write: Moonlight Bay Resort, 4151 Moonlight Bay Trail,
Traverse City, MI 49686.

	1 Bedroom	2 Bedroom	3 Bedroom
Summer Weekly *	$380-$520	$560-$595	$750

* Off-season rates lower

HAROLD MYERS   **(616) 946-3909**
                                          COTTAGE

Three bedrooms, ranch-style cottage with kitchen, dining area, living room
w/brick fireplace, screened porch facing the lake, 2 car attached garage on
paved road. Located in a quiet and very private area. Good fishing and
swimming. Includes bedding, towels, CATV, rowboat and dock. $100 non-
refundable deposit after May 1st.

Weekly $550   (Seasonal rates)

146

WILKINS LANDING   **(616) 946-5219**
ROLF & KATHY SCHLIESS   COTTAGE

Quiet, private, secluded, this private residence enjoys 225 ft. of beautiful Spider Lake frontage with dock, paddle boat and pontoon boat. Fully furnished (except linens) with fieldstone fireplace, equipped kitchen and more! Available year around. 4 bedrooms, 2 baths, sleeps 11.

Weekly (summer) $960/10 people

WINDJAMMER RESORT   **(616) 946-8466**
PAUL KNAPP   COTTAGES

Clean, comfortable, rustic cottages are completely furnished for housekeeping. These 7 cottages have 1-3 bedrooms, bathroom with shower, kitchen, living room and outside deck. Kitchen fully equipped. All newly carpeted and painted. Pillows and blankets are provided (bring your own linens and towels). Sandy beach, 160 ft. frontage. Boats/canoe available. No pets.

Weekly $325-$470

SUTTONS BAY

THE COUNTRY HOUSE   **(616) 271-4478 • (616) 941-1010**
VACATION HOME

Fully furnished house in Suttons Bay offers A/C and 2 bedrooms (sleeps up to 4). It is centrally located to Lake Michigan and Lake Leelanau.

Weekly $375-$550

OPEN WINDOWS BED AND BREAKFAST   **(616) 271-4300 • (800) 520-3722**
DON & NORMA BLUMENSCHINE   BED & BREAKFAST

This 100 year old home, reminiscent of a bygone era, is beautifully furnished with family heirlooms and antiques. Walk the beach, swim, ride our bikes, visit the unique shops in Suttons Bay, or simply relax beside an open window enjoying the view. 3 rooms. Open year around.

Daily $70-$90

THOMPSONVILLE

CRYSTAL MOUNTAIN RESORT   **(800) 968-7686 • (616) 378-2000**
MAIN OFFICE RENTALS   CONDOS/RESORT HOMES

In addition to its motel, Crystal Mountain Resort offers deluxe condos and resort home rentals. Features in-room Jacuzzi, full service dining room, live entertainment, indoor and outdoor pools, fitness center, 27-hole golf course

MICHIGAN COTTAGES • CHALETS • CONDOS • B&B'S

CRYSTAL MOUNTAIN RESORT (continued...)
and clay tennis courts. Great skiing w/23 downhill ski slopes and 30 kms. cross-country ski trails, night skiing, rentals, lessons. Summer and winter children's programs. 28 miles from Traverse City.

Daily $60-$396 (assumes 2 people)

TORCH LAKE

JANE BLIZMAN   **(810) 644-7288 • (616) 264-5228**
                                                      COTTAGES
Two cottages offered, on /800 ft. of Torch Lake amid 25 acres of woods and fields. Features antique furnishings and snooker table. Each cottage has fireplace, color TV, stereo, dishwasher, microwave, washer/dryer, all linens and cookware. Also includes dock w/lift, picnic table and grill.

	1 Bedroom	5 Bedroom	
Weekly*	$1,200	$1,500	* Prices based on up to 4 people

RICH & JANE CARLSON   **(513) 579-0473**
                                            VACATION HOME

A lovely, fully equipped, 3 bedroom/2 bath home is available for rent year around. It is conveniently located within 1/2 hour drive of Charlevoix and Traverse City— close to excellent skiing and golf courses. A fireplace and 2 car garage w/remote control door make it cozy and comfortable. A large 1 acre, beautifully landscaped lot with 100 ft. of lake frontage offers great views. In warmer months, enjoy the sun deck equipped w/gas grill and private dock.

	June	July/August
Weekly	$900	$1,200

Editor's Note: Spacious and well landscaped lot — a real home-away-from home. Sloping grounds take you to pebbled beach. See our review in this edition!

TORCH LAKE BED & BREAKFAST   **(616) 331-6424**
JACK & PATTI FINDLAY   BED & BREAKFAST
Renovated 19th century Victorian uses period furniture. European lace and stained glass. The hilltop setting provides exceptional views of Torch Lake. Surprising Alden delights with gourmet dining, boutiques and is located in the center of Michigan's Gold Coast of golf. Open Memorial weekend through Labor Day weekend. 3 rooms.

Daily $65-$85

TORCHLIGHT RESORT   **(616) 544-8263**
ROBERT & GLENDA KNOTT   **COTTAGES**

Six cottages w/150 ft. frontage on Torch Lake (part of the Chain of Lakes). Features sandy beach, playground, excellent boat harbor, beautiful sunsets. Located between Traverse City and Charlevoix. Near excellent golf courses and fine restaurants. Open May thru October. No pets.

Weekly $440-$600 (Off-season rates available)
Editor's Note: Friendly owners, clean cottages in a lovely setting make this one a great retreat! See our review in this edition.

TORCH TIMBERS BED & BREAKFAST   **(616) 331-4050**
TINA & DAN MORDEN   **BED & BREAKFAST**

Exquisite 1930's 2-1/2 story grand lodge, situated on over 1900 ft. of private Torch Lake shoreline. Large great room to gather in. Four split natural stone fireplaces, game room and more. Outside activities include: nature trail, putting green, boat dockage, picnic area, and other outdoor games. Full breakfast. Private and shared baths. 5 rooms. No smoking.

Daily $100-$160

TORCH TIP RESORT   **(616) 599-2313**
KIM & LAURA SCHMIDT   **COTTAGES**
Located on beautiful Torch Lake, this resort offers 12 cottages—1 room (studio style) or 2 bedrooms. Features include swimming beach, swim platform, game room, tackle shop, volleyball, and shuffleboard. Pontoons and Jet skis available. Boat included. Open April 1 through Dec. 1. No pets.

Weekly $325-$600

TRAVERSE CITY

BOWERS HARBOR BED & BREAKFAST   **(616) 223-7869**
                                               BED & BREAKFAST

1870 fully remodeled country farmhouse with private sandy beach is located in the Old Mission Peninsula. Open year around. Enjoy a gourmet breakfast on the wrap-around porch overlooking Bowers Harbor. 3 rooms w/private baths.

Daily $85-$110

MICHIGAN COTTAGES • CHALETS • CONDOS • B&B'S

CHÂTEAU CHANTAL BED & BREAKFAST
(616) 223-4110
BED & BREAKFAST

Retreat to the Old World in this *new*, fully operational vineyard, winery and B&B. Set on a beautifully landscaped, scenic hill in the Old Mission Peninsula, this grand estate features an opulent wine tasting room and 3 delightful guest rooms (includes 2 suites) with private baths. Handicap accessible. Full breakfast.

Daily $95-$125 (assumes 2 people - $25 for each additional person)

CIDER HOUSE BED & BREAKFAST
(616) 947-2833
BED & BREAKFAST

Enjoy cider and Scottish shortbread overlooking the apple blossoms. Pick your own apples in fall. Contemporary country inn is only minutes from downtown Traverse City. Beautiful oak floors, fireplace, canopy beds. Country style breakfast. 5 rooms w/private baths.

Daily $55-$75

THE GRAINERY
(616) 946-8325
BED & BREAKFAST

Relax in this 1892 Country Gentleman's home! Located on 10 lovely acres. Decorated in the country Victorian tradition. Coffee pot, fridge, CATV and outdoor hot tub along with 2 golf greens and a pond. Full country breakfast.

Daily $45-$95

JIM & CONNIE LEGATO
(616) 946-3842
HOME

Well maintained older home, 3 bedrooms, sleeps 9. Features cable TV, phone, and fully equipped kitchen. Linens provided. Quiet in-town location 2 blocks from swimming beach on Grand Traverse Bay and 4 blocks from town. Available year around. Pets welcome.

Weekly $550

RANCH RUDOLF
(616) 947-9529
LODGE/BUNKHOUSE

Entertainment Friday and Saturday nights. Restaurant and lounge with fireplace. Enjoy the hay rides, sleigh rides, river fishing, backpacking, horseshoes, hiking, tennis, swimming pool, badminton, volleyball and a children's playground. Visa and MC accepted.

Call for Rates

TALL SHIP MALABAR
(616) 941-2000
BED & BREAKFAST

Unique "floating" B&B! This large traditional sailing vessel offers overnight accommodations along with a 2-1/2 hour sunset sail w/picnic dinner and a hearty breakfast! Come join the crew for a special evening on this 105 ft., two-masted topsail schooner. May-Sept.

Daily $95-$175 (children 8-12 $45)

150

WEST BAY

La Petite Maison Sur L'eau
Theda Connell
(616) 386-5462
Vacation Home

Intimate, charming, attractively furnished, this 1 bedroom property features a large window overlooking the lawn to water's edge. Secluded, ideal for honeymooners or small family. Safe swimming, hiking, walking.

Call for Rates

Shel & Sherry Larkby
(616) 946-8010
Cottages

1st Cottage *Bayside:* Remodeled in 1990 and features 2 bedrooms (sleeps 4) and includes microwave, phone, CATV, VCR and linens. No pets.

Weekly $425

2nd Cottage: Charming Victorian Gothic Farmhouse, also remodeled, features 4 bedrooms (sleeps 8). Includes microwave, 2 full baths, CATV, VCR, phone, dishwasher, disposal, washer/dryer and linens. No pets.

Weekly $1,200-$1,400

Lerew's Cottage
Christa Eaton
(219) 875-1241 • (800) 234-0227 (ext. 107)
Home

Three bedroom home (sleeps 8) on 200 ft. of private sandy beach near Old Mission Light House. It can easily be shared by 2 families. Includes dishwasher, washer/dryer. Garage apartment w/bath included for additional fee. Shallow water, safe swimming. Tennis and docking nearby.

Weekly $1,200-$1,400

Ronald Mallek
(616) 386-5041 • (201) 766-7045
Cottage

This charming, 1 bedroom (sleeps 3), English country cottage features a private patio, many gardens and sandy beach. Fully furnished with fireplace, equipped kitchen. No pets/smoking.

Weekly $500

Private Cottage
Ken
(616) 947-5948
Cottage

One bedroom rental, large living room, private sandy beach, Grand Traverse Bay. Three blocks from downtown, 1 block to City tennis courts. Completely furnished, includes TV, microwave, canoe, rowboat. Please provide own linens. $100 deposit.

Weekly $700   (Cherry Festival Week $800)

Editor's Note: Small, private cottage with all the conveniences. Quiet setting, large windows with spectacular sunsets make this one appealing! See our review in this edition!

MICHIGAN COTTAGES • CHALETS • CONDOS • B&B'S

STRAWBERRY HILL HOUSE (616) 228-6963
MARGO ABBOTT WATERFRONT HOME
Peaceful and charming. Secluded 4 bedroom log home, south of
Suttons Bay. Rustic but refined — with great views over orchards
and water. Screened porch, stone fireplace, antiques, fully carpeted,
1-1/2 baths. Stairs down bluff to scenic private beach. Furnished
except for linens. No pets/smoking.

Weekly $800-$1,000

THE VICTORIANA 1898 (616) 929-1009
BED & BREAKFAST
Visitors to this Victorian style B&B are greeted with exquisitely crafted tiled
fireplaces, oak staircase, gazebo and carriage house. Located in a quiet, historic
district, the lodging is close to West Bay, downtown. "Very Special" breakfasts
are served each morning. 3 rooms.

Daily $55-$75

WYNDENROK ON THE BAY (616) 386-5462
THEDA CONNELL VACATION HOME
Three bedroom, 1920's nostalgia summer home, on quiet, private, and wooded
lot w/166 ft. bay frontage. Beautiful view from its 3 screened porches. French
doors lead to outside balcony which overlooks Grand Traverse Bay.
Comfortably furnished w/piano. A massive stone fireplace adds to the
ambiance of the home. No pets/smoking.

Weekly $850   Call for Lower Rates May/June/Sept./Oct.

CADILLAC & ONEKAMA

The Cadillac area is an excellent stop for fishing and water sports
enthusiasts with its two lakes (Cadillac and Mitchell) within its
city limits and many other lakes not far away. Wild and tame game is
abundant at Johnny's Wild Game and Fish Park which also stocks its waters
with plenty of trout! In February, come and enjoy the North American
Snowmobile Festival!

For additional information on Activities in the area, contact:

Cadillac Area Chamber of Commerce
200 Lake Street, Cadillac, MI 49601
(800) 548-9176 (MI only) • (616) 775-9776

CADILLAC

ESSENMACHER'S BED & BREAKFAST
DOUG & VICKIE ESSENMACHER

(616) 775-3828
BED & BREAKFAST

Imagine a different breakfast every day of your stay! To be pampered with flowers and candy in your room! A blazing fire in a stone fireplace and a hot beverage to warm you. Each guest's stay is very special. There are 2 guest rooms with a spectacular view of Lake Mitchell. The lake is great for fishing, boating, swimming and sea planning. Nearby are miles of groomed snowmobile trails, x-country ski paths, downhill skiing, fine dining and 15 min. from ski resorts.

Daily $50-$55

ONEKAMA

LAKE MICHIGAN CHALET HIDEAWAY
DONNA

(312) 943-7565
CHALET

An elegant, spacious 3 bedroom, 3 bath fully furnished home on Lake Michigan. This 3,500 sq. ft. home features fireplaces, a fully equipped kitchen with dishwasher and microwave, living room/dining room, CATV, VCR, CD stereo and sauna. Lake and sunset viewing deck in addition to a large attached deck with BBQ pit. Private setting. Weekly maid service and linens included. Winterized. No pets. Weekend and monthly rentals.

Weekly $1,200-$1,500

REGION 6

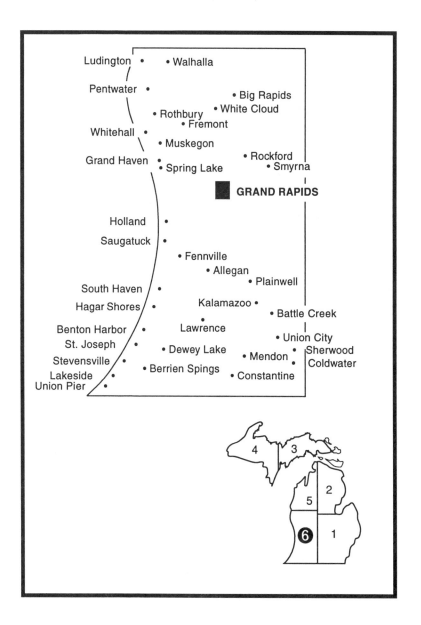

Ludington •   • Walhalla

Pentwater •

• Big Rapids
• White Cloud
• Rothbury
• Fremont

Whitehall •   • Muskegon

Grand Haven •   • Rockford
• Spring Lake   • Smyrna

■ **GRAND RAPIDS**

Holland •

Saugatuck •

• Fennville
• Allegan
• Plainwell

South Haven •
Hagar Shores •   Kalamazoo •
• Battle Creek

Benton Harbor •   Lawrence
St. Joseph •   • Dewey Lake   • Union City
Stevensville •   • Mendon   Sherwood
Lakeside •   • Berrien Spings   Coldwater
Union Pier •   • Constantine

REGION 6

This unique region offers a variety of things to see and do. Where else would you find a city that can claim to have over 450 lakes! It also boats over 100,000 acres of nature preserves, sand dunes, great fishing, golf, wonderful beaches, winter sports and one of the most scenic and elaborate bike trail systems in Michigan.

Sometimes referred to as "The Riviera of the Midwest" because of its land and climate, the area produces some of Michigan's finest premium wines. Fore something a little different in this orchard country, why not stop at the annual Cherry Pit Spitting Championship! You can relax watching the world's largest Music Fountain or add a new twist to fishing with "Party Boat Fishing". If you feel daring, the area is also known for hang gliding.

You can spend the day with great shopping, theaters and double decker bus rides. There are plenty of festivals to enjoy, such as the famous Tulip Festival and Cereal Festival with the world's longest breakfast table.

Maybe you want to skip back in time. Try their museums or many historic districts which incorporate more than 1500 historic houses on 27 square blocks.

If you enjoy traditional vacation fun with a twist, this is the place!

LUDINGTON • GRAND RAPIDS • HOLLAND & SURROUNDING AREAS

COVERS: BIG RAPIDS • FENNVILLE • FREMONT • GRAND HAVEN •
MUSKEGON • PENTWATER • ROCKFORD • ROTHBURY • SMYRNA •
SPRING LAKE • WALHALLA • WHITE CLOUD • WHITEHALL

Nestled between Lake Michigan and the Allegan State Forest is **Fennville**. This community is surrounded by vineyards, such as Fenn Valley Vineyards. Take a tour and sample the premium grape and natural fruit wines.

A boardwalk, stretching for 2-/2 miles from downtown **Grand Haven** to its pier, is bordered by shops and eateries and many sandy beaches. Be sure to visit Moser's, a unique shop filled with dried-flower arrangements and country style decorations. For a grand tour, hop on board the Harbor Steamer. For a spectacular sight, see the World's Largest Musical Fountain and visit Michigan's second largest zoo which has 150 species of animals, an aquarium, herpetarium, and more!

Grand Rapids, a unique blend of old and new, the city has many activities to keep you busy! Heritage Hill contains almost 100 historical homes. You'll also want to visit the John Ball Zoological Gardens, Roger B. Chaffe Planetarium, and the Voigt House, a Victorian home built in 1895.

People from all over come to **Holland's** May "Tulip Time Festival", but there is much to see here throughout the year. Dutch Village should not be missed — and don't leave without seeing the Wooden Shoe Factory or Windmill Island!

Ludington features one of the largest charter-fishing fleets on Lake Michigan and is well known for its coho and salmon population. A piece of history can be found at the White Pine Village, a 19th century pioneering town. Bike through 22 miles of nature in Michigan's first linear state park, the Hart-Montage Bicycle Trail State Park. Several notable restaurants in the area include *P.M. Steamers* for a good view of marina activities or *Gibbs Country House* to indulge in their truly sticky, sticky buns and well prepared American cuisine in a family atmosphere!

For a change of pace, enjoy the New England charm of **Pentwater**, with its cozy cafes and double-decker bus. Build a sand castle in the Silver Lake State Park which features a huge "sandbox" with 450 acres of dunes for off-road vehicles and 750 acres for pedestrians only!

LUDINGTON • GRAND RAPIDS • HOLLAND & SURROUNDING AREAS

(continued...)

Hungry? Try some of Pentwater's unique restaurants: *Historic Nickerson Inn* for a warm and charming atmosphere (reservations requested); the *Village Pub* for casual pizza and fish sandwiches and evening entertainment of comedy or jazz; the *Antler Bar* known for their special burrito; and *Gull Landing* serves up excellent steak and seafood.

With plenty to do in this great lake playground, you will find the atmosphere relaxed, the people friendly, and the scenery beautiful.

For additional information on events and activities in the area contact:

Ludington Area CVB
5827 W. U.S. 10, P.O. Box 160
Ludington, MI 49431
(800) 542-4600

Holland CVB
150 W. Eighth Street
Holland, MI 49423
(616) 396-4221 • (800) 622-2770

Grand Rapids-Kent County CVB
245 Monroe, NW
Grand Rapids, MI 49503
(800) 678-9859 • (616) 459-8287

Pentwater Chamber of Commerce
P.O. Box 614
Pentwater, MI 49449
(616) 869-4150

BIG RAPIDS

HILLVIEW RESORT   **(616) 796-5928**
GREG/PATTI BEDUHN   **CABINS**
Seven knotty pine cabins located on Hillview Lake, have 1-3 bedrooms, space heater, shower, picnic table, fire pit, and screened in porches. Kitchens fully equipped, double beds have pillows and a blanket. Great fishing (blue gill, sunfish, bass, pike), 5 row boats, 2 canoes and 1 paddle boat, included with rental. Sandy beach and swimming area. Boat landing if you would like to bring your own boat.

Weekly $225-$275   Daily $30-$50

FENNVILLE

THE KINGSLEY HOUSE   **(616) 561-6425**
DAVID & SHIRLEY WITT   **BED & BREAKFAST**
1886 elegant Queen Anne Victorian B&B. Featured in <u>Innsider Magazine</u>, rated as a "Top Fifty Inn" in America by <u>Inn Times</u>. AAA approved, it is located near Holland and Saugatuck and has sandy beaches, x-country skiing, bicycles. Private baths, whirlpool/bath. Get away honeymoon suite. Beautiful surroundings, family antiques. Full breakfast. A/C. 7 rooms.

Daily $75-$125

HIDDEN POND BED & BREAKFAST   **(616) 561-2491**
PRISCILLA & LARRY FUERST   **BED & BREAKFAST**
Accommodations of quiet traditional elegance. Two bedrooms with private baths, plus five common rooms. 28 acres of private ravined grounds with wildlife and pond. Selected by <u>Frommer B&B North America Guidebook</u> as one of the "50 Best B&B Homes in America". 2 rooms.

Daily $64-$110

FREMONT

GERBER HOUSE BED & BREAKFAST   **(616) 924-2829**
ROMAN & MARY ANN SCHEIDEL   **BED & BREAKFAST**
This home was built by the originators of Gerber Baby Food. 80 acres next to Fremont Lake. Casual elegance, spacious grounds, indoor pool, tennis, walking trails, x-country skiing, fishing, canoe, paddle boat, nearby golf courses, king beds, Jacuzzi suite, full breakfast, group facilities. "Our Commitment is to your comfort." (Not affiliated w/Gerber Prod. Co.)

Daily $70-$125

GRAND HAVEN

BOYDEN HOUSE INN BED & BREAKFAST   **(616) 846-3538**
CORRIE & BEREND SNOEYER   **BED & BREAKFAST**
Our 1874 Victorian Home, its eclectic decor representing our varied interests; welcomes guests to cozy rooms, delightful breakfasts, books, flowers, walks on beaches and boardwalks. An exciting day may be concluded with whirlpool baths or a fireplace room, creating a memory worth recalling.

Daily $75-$85

MICHIGAN COTTAGES • CHALETS • CONDOS • B&B'S

GRAND RAPIDS & EAST GRAND RAPIDS

CHICAGO POINT RESORT   **(616) 795-7216 • (517) 321-4562**
COTTAGES

Located between Kalamazoo and Grand Rapids, on the southeast side of Gun Lake. The resort is convenient to Yankee Springs Recreation Area which offers 5,000 acres of country wilderness trails and natural beauty. Al Capone was said to have paid a visit here! The resort features 2, 3 and 4 bedroom cottages, fully furnished and equipped (provide you own blankets, sheets and towels), private beach, fishing docks and picnic area. Rowboats, canoes, paddle boat and sailboat available for rent. No pets.

Weekly $450-$750

BRUCE & LAUREL YOUNG   **(616) 942-6568**
VACATION HOME

Lake Michigan cottage located on 100 feet of low bank sandy beach. Four bedrooms (sleeps 10), 2 baths, fireplace, fully equipped kitchen, heat, bed linens provided, deck, gas grill. Limit of 3 car parking, private association. No pets.

Weekly $800 (May/June/Sept) $1,500 (July/Aug)

HOLLAND

DUTCH COLONIAL INN B&B   **(616) 396-0461 • (616) 396-3664**
PAT & BOB ELENBAAS   **BED & BREAKFAST**
1928 Dutch Colonial Inn features elegant decor with 1930 furnishings and heirloom antiques. All guest rooms have tiled private baths with the optional use of whirlpool tub for 2. Honeymoon suites available for that "Special Getaway". Includes: shopping, Hope College, bike paths, x-country ski trails and beaches. Business people welcome. A/C. 5 rooms.

Daily $70-$125

EDGEWOOD BEACH   **(313) 692-3941**
GERALYN PLAKMEYER   COTTAGE

Located just north of Holland, in Beach Front Association. Home has 2 bedrooms, 1 bath, fully furnished, equipped kitchen, fireplace, central heat. 150' back from Lake Michigan, stairway to long sandy beach complete with sunsets and fire pit. Provide your own linens. Available June to Sept. No pets!

Weekly $500

160

NORTH SHORE INN (616) 394-9050
BEVERLY & KURT VAN GENDEREN BED & BREAKFAST
An elegant historical estate, overlooking Lake Macatawa. Three guest bedrooms, furnished with antiques and handmade quilts. A three course, home
cooked breakfast is served on the porch or formal dining room. Guests may
choose king, queen or double beds, private or shared bath.

Call for Rates

THE OLD HOLLAND INN (616) 396-6601
DAVE PLAGGEMARS BED & BREAKFAST
Nationally registered B&B features 10 ft. ceiling, brass fixtures, stained glass
windows and a lovely brass-inlaid fireplace. Antiques, fresh flowers decorate
each air conditioned room. Enjoy special house-blend coffee, fresh muffins,
fruit and cheese plates each morning.

Daily $40-$75

THE PARSONAGE 1908 (616) 396-1316
BONNIE VERWYS BED & BREAKFAST
Close to Hope College and the Convention Center, this elegant European
style lodging offers its guests 4 air conditioned rooms (2 private and 2 shared
baths) and a full breakfast each morning. Convenient to beaches, boating,
x-country skiing, bike trails, theater, fine dining, antique shops and art gallery. No pet/smoking.

Daily $60-$75 (sgl) $80-$95 (dbl)

LUDINGTON

BED & BREAKFAST AT LUDINGTON (616) 843-9768
GRACE & ROBERT SCHNEIDER BED & BREAKFAST
Hills, dales, woods, pond and trails, big breakfast, big hot tub, barn loft
hideaway. Children invited. Toboggans, snowshoes provided. 3 miles out of
Ludington. 3 double rooms.

Daily $40-$60

DOLL HOUSE INN (616) 843-2286
JOE & BARBARA GEROVAC BED & BREAKFAST
Gracious 1900 American Foursquare. Seven rooms including bridal suite with
whirlpool tub for two. Enclosed porch, smoke and pet free, adult
accommodations, full Heart Smart breakfast. A/C. Corporate rates, bicycles,
x-country skiing. Walk to beach, town, transportation to car ferry and air
port. Surrounded by antiques, modern facilities. Special weekend package.

Daily $55-$95

MICHIGAN COTTAGES • CHALETS • CONDOS • B&B'S

THE INN AT LUDINGTON
DIANE SHIELDS
(616) 845-7055
BED & BREAKFAST

Elegant accommodations in this 103 year old Queen Anne Victorian. Lovingly decorated throughout, with family heirlooms and cherished collectibles. Also features a bridal suite, fireplaces, family suite. Breakfast here, is an event — not an after thought. Walk to shops, restaurants, beach and marina. 6 rooms.

Daily $55-$85

THE LAMPLIGHTER B & B
JUDY & HEINZ BARTRAM
(616) 843-9792
BED & BREAKFAST

Victorian Style, European elegance and American comfort are the hallmarks of "The Lamplighter Bed and Breakfast" Your stay in our individually decorated rooms with queen size beds, private baths, A/C, CATV and phones; will be the most relaxing possible. Our newest room features a whirlpool for two. All rooms as well as the common areas-parlor, living room and dining room — are decorated with original art and antiques. Full gourmet breakfasts are served either in our dining room or outdoors on the deck in the gazebo. Our premises are "protected" by our Cocker Spaniel "Freddie".

Daily $65-$105

PARKVIEW COTTAGES
DENNIS & JILL
(616) 843-4445
COTTAGES

Nestled in a grove of shade trees only a block from the park on Lake Michigan, these cottages sleep from 2-6. Each features a private bath with ceramic tiled shower, fully equipped kitchen, gas heat, CATV (w/HBO), fieldstone fireplace (firewood included), and grill.

Call for Rates

TWIN POINTS RESORT
JIM & BARB HUSTED
(616) 843-9434
COTTAGES

10 cottages (1-3 bedrooms) rest on 2 wooded bluffs overlooking lovely Hamlet Lake. Walk down to large and sandy swimming beach. Boaters can back their trailers down with ease. Moor your boat in covered docks. Motors and boats available for rent. Cottages are fully furnished and equipped. Most have knotty pine interiors. Close to Ludington State Park.

Call for Rates

WILLOW BY THE LAKE RESORT
GORDON/DAVID BETCHER & MARTIN LUTZENKIRCHEN
(616) 843-2904
COTTAGES

Attractive, clean, 1 and 2 bedroom housekeeping cottages with equipped kitchens. Guests provide linens/towels. Beautiful view of sand dunes and sunsets from east shore of Hamlin Lake. Sandy beach/play areas for children. Dockage/boat rentals available. Open May-October. No pets.

Weekly $285-$370

MUSKEGON

VACATION HOMES   **(616) 842-5716**
CAROLYN MILLER   VACATION HOMES
Beautifully decorated home on Lake Michigan with adjoining efficiency. Cottage sleeps 5 and efficiency 4. Both have supplied kitchens, baths and linens. Main cottage has dishwasher, washer, dryer and fireplace. Rented together or separately. Private beach. Available May-Dec. No pets.

Weekly   Main Cottage $450   Efficiency $400   Loft $400

PENTWATER

THE CANDLEWYCK HOUSE B&B   **(616) 869-5967**
JOHN & MARY JO NEIDOW   BED & BREAKFAST
This 1868 home offers a unique and comfortable place for families. Each room (2 with private bath) is individually furnished with Americana and folk art from our popular gift shop, The Painted Pony Mercantile. Walk to shops, beaches and pier fishing. Bikes, skis and sports equipment on premise. 4 rooms. Full country breakfast.

Daily $50-$70

HISTORIC NICKERSON INN   **(616) 869-6731**
HENRY & GRETCHEN SHIPARSKI   BED & BREAKFAST
Serving guests with "Special Hospitality" since 1914. On a bluff overlooking Lake Michigan. Completely renovated, all rooms have private baths and A/C. Two Jacuzzi suites with fireplaces and balconies overlooking Lake Michigan. Two blocks to beach and shopping district. Casual fine dining, cocktails. Consider romantic getaways, workshops retreats, marriage encounters. 12 rooms. Private bath.

Daily $75-$150

PENTWATER INN   **(616) 869-5909**
SUE & DICK HAND   BED & BREAKFAST
Charming 1880's home, full of antiques and teddy bears in quaint Pentwater. Beautiful beach, international shopping, charter fishing, all within walking distance. Relax in our hot tub and enjoy a beautiful buffet breakfast with homemade pastries. No children under 10. No smoking, no pets. 5 rooms.

Daily $55-$60

MICHIGAN COTTAGES • CHALETS • CONDOS • B&B'S

PERKINS PLACE (616) 869-8751
M.A. PERKINS COTTAGE/APARTMENT

On Lake Michigan, in a quiet residential area between Pentwater and Ludington. Clean sandy beaches are good for sunbathing and walking. Each rental unit has 2 bedrooms (limit 4), bathroom, living/dining area and fully equipped kitchen. Bring sheets and towels. Cleaning products are supplied. $100 deposit.

Weekly $450

ROCKFORD

VILLAGE ROSE BED & BREAKFAST (616) 866-7041
BROOKS & NICK FILONOW BED & BREAKFAST

This Victorian Era farmhouse is located on a tree lined street in downtown Rockford, one of West Michigan's most pleasant old mill towns. The newly decorated second floor guest quarters offers a private kitchen and sitting area, brass beds, fresh flowers in every room and special breakfast. 3 rooms.

Rates $35-$60

ROTHBURY

DOUBLE JJ RESORT (616) 894-4444
HOTEL/CONDOS

Exceptional horseback riding, championship golf, archery, rifle range, swimming, boating and a whole lot more at this adult-exclusive ranch/resort. Rooms vary from basic sleeping rooms to luxury condos and hotel rooms. Activities are too numerous to mention. Entertainment nightly. Price includes all activities, entertainment, and meals!

Weekend $209-$309 Weekly $539-$889

Editor's Note: The word bored never happens at Double JJ — there's so much to do! Excellent horseback riding, wonderful golf course, beautiful grounds and friendly ranch hands too...Yee-haw! See our Review this issue.

164

SMYRNA

DOUBLE 'R' RANCH RESORT   **(616) 794-0520**
                          CHALETS/BUNK HOUSE MOTEL

Lets go tubing on the Flat River! Great fishing too — pike & small mouth bass. Shuffleboard, volleyball, horseback riding, golf, canoeing, hay rides. Each chalet has electric stove, refrigerator and all dishes. Chalets rent by week. For overnight stays, try the rustic western atmosphere of the Bunk House Motel.

	May, June, Sept.	July & Aug.
Chalet	$290	$370
	Daily	Weekly
Motel	$33-$48	$190-$280

SPRING LAKE

SEASCAPE BED & BREAKFAST   **(616) 842-8409**
SUSAN MEYER   **BED & BREAKFAST**

On a private Lake Michigan beach. Enjoy the hospitality and "country living" ambiance of our nautical lake shore home. Full homemade breakfast served in gathering room (with fieldstone fireplace) or on sun deck. Either offers a panoramic view of Grand Haven Harbor. Stroll or x-country ski on dune land nature trails. 3 rooms.

Daily $75-$90 (Special rates Sun-Thur.)

WALHALLA

BAROTHY LODGE   **(616) 898-2340**
PAUL/CATHY   **CHALETS**

Situated on the Pere Marquette River, in the Manistee National Forest, these luxury units offer 1-8 bedrooms, 2-3 bathrooms (linens provided), with fireplaces (wood furnished), completely equipped kitchen. Larger units have pool tables and Jacuzzi. Fish for chinook and coho salmon, rainbow, brown, brook, and steelhead trout. No pets.

Call for Rates

WHITE CLOUD

THE CROW'S NEST   **(616) 689-0088**
JOYCE & DICK BILLINGSLEY   **BED & BREAKFAST**

Experience the warmth and charm of our renovated home in a country setting located on the banks of the White River. Stroll by the river's edge, inspect our barn, pick blueberries. Enjoy a full breakfast served in the formal dining room or the glass/screen enclosed porch overlooking the river. We have 3 guest rooms with queen beds, 1 with private bath.

Daily $45-$65

WHITEHALL

MICHILINDA BEACH RESORT   **(616) 893-1895**
     COTTAGES/LODGE ROOMS

Modified American Plan resort with weekly activities and plenty to do. Well groomed grounds on scenic location. In operation almost 60 years. Cottages and lodge rooms offer private baths and most with sitting areas (no kitchens). Many rooms with lake views. Prices include breakfast and lunch. 49 rooms available. Open May to early October. No pets.

Lodge Rooms	Daily	$130-$161	Weekly	$680-$,1025
Cottages	Daily	$210 (and up)	Weekly	$1,075-$1,310

Editor's Note: Well groomed, picturesque resort with plenty to keep families and couples very busy. Rooms comfortable and clean. See our review in this edition!

TIMEKEEPER'S INN & CLOCK SHOP   **(616) 894-5169**
GERDA MEYER   **BED & BREAKFAST**

All the comforts of a true European home awaits gue Open May-Nov. 3 rooms with private baths.

Daily $75-$90

SAUGATUCK • KALAMAZOO • BENTON HARBOR • UNION PIER & SURROUNDING

COVERS: ALLEGAN • BATTLE CREEK • BERRIEN SPRINGS • COLDWATER • CONSTANTINE • DEWEY LAKE • HAGAR SHORES • LAKESIDE • LAWRENCE • MENDON • PLAINWELL • ST. JOSEPH • SHERWOOD • SOUTH HAVEN • STEVENSVILLE • UNION CITY • UNION PIER

Battle Creek, home of the cereal pioneers W. K. Kellogg and C. W. Post, has given this city the name of "Cereal Capital of the World". It is also the site of Fort Custer National Cemetery and the International Hot-Air Balloon Championship which last for 8 days in June.

Kalamazoo — how very diverse! Whatever you wish to do or see is here. From Victorian homes and quaint inns, tours, classic cars & aircraft, museums, theaters, sports or historic districts. For galleries and antique shops stop at **Lakeside**.

Relax amid historic homes, bed and breakfast inns, fragrant orchards, boat cruises, dune rides, golf courses and antique shops in **Saugatuck**. Take a cruise on the Queen of Saugatuck, a 67 ft. stern wheel riverboat, or ride across the sand dunes. Take a tour of the Tabor Hill Wine Port, and taste Michigan premium wines.

South Haven not only prides itself as the "Blueberry Capital of the World" it is also one of our major yachting and sport fishing ports. Explore the many parks, hike over the sand dunes or, if you dare, go hang gliding in the Warren Dunes State Park just south of **St. Joseph**. In the fall, harvest festivals and color tours are popular. Ice fishing and skiing attract enthusiasts in the winter. May brings The Blossom Time Festival celebrated for over 80 years, In mid-July is the Venetian Festival—the lakefront park and Lake Boulevard become a giant midway. You won't want to miss this one!

Getting hungry yet! Try out *Jenny's* on Lakeshore Road (between New Buffalo and Union Pier). Creatively prepared food and homey atmosphere featuring Great Lakes Indian art and high-beamed ceiling with skylights make this a worthwhile stop! Also, *Schu's Grill & Bar* on Lake Boulevard (St. Joseph) prepares excellent meals — their Blackout Cake is a wonderful treat! We understand the *North Beach Inn* serve's up very memorable blueberry pancakes or waffles! Try the *Three Pelican's* (South Haven) casual dining on the water.

For additional information about events and activities in these areas contact:

Southwestern Michigan Tourist Council
2300 Pipestone Road, Benton Harbor, MI 49022
(616) 925-6301

ALLEGAN

ALVA SPRIENSMA   **(616) 538-2575**
                                                              COTTAGE

Modern lakefront (110 ft. frontage) cottage on Miner Lake near Allegan (Southwestern MI). Miner Lake covers 350 acres, excellent for fishing, swimming, skiing. 2 baths, 2 bedrooms, queen sofa sleeper (sleeps 6). Paddle boat, raft included. Excellent beach. Cooking utensils, dishes provided. Bring linens. No pets. Available spring/summer.

Weekly $400   Weekend $175

BATTLE CREEK

GREENCREST MANOR   **(616) 962-8633**
TOM & KATHY VAN DAFF   **BED & BREAKFAST**

This grand French Normandy mansion situated on the highest elevation of St. Mary's Lake is constructed of sandstone, slate and copper. Formal gardens include fountains and cut stone urns. A/C. Private baths. 5 rooms. Featured, in "Country Inns Magazine" as "Inn of the Month" and Top 12 Inns of North America of 1992.

Daily $75-$170

BERRIEN SPRINGS

PENNELLWOOD RESORT   **(616) 473-2511**
JACK & PAT DAVIS   COTTAGES

One price includes everything—meals, lodging, recreation and entertainment. 39 cottages have 2 and 3 bedrooms. Bring beach towels, life jackets & tennis racquets. Enjoy pontoon rides, volleyball, softball, shuffleboard, archery, tubing, wine tasting and Monte Carlo night. Reservations required. $125 deposit. No pets.

Call for Rates

COLDWATER

BATAVIA INN   **(517) 278-5146**
FRED & ALMA MARQUARDT   COUNTRY INN

An 1872 Italianate country inn with original massive wood-work, high ceilings and restful charm. Near antique and outlet shopping, lakes, parks, museums and recreation. Seasonal decorations a specialty. In-ground pool. Guest pampering is the Innkeepers' goal. 5 rooms.

Daily $59-$99

Chicago Pike Inn   **(517) 279-8744**
Rebecca Schultz   **BED & BREAKFAST**

Turn of the century reformed Colonial Mansion adorned with antiques from the Victorian era. Six guest rooms in main house, two with whirlpools in Carriage House, all with private baths. Formal dining room, library, and reception room feature sweeping cherry staircase and parquet floors. Full country breakfast and refreshments.

Daily $80-$165

CONSTANTINE

"Our Olde House" B&B Inn   **(800) 435-5365**
Sandy & Jim Withers   **BED & BREAKFAST**

Located in Historical Village near antique centers. Inn features antique fireplace mantels, European antiques, in-ground pool. Rooms offers private bath (two w/ Jacuzzis) and fireplaces. Full breakfast. Near Amish Shipshewana, Indiana. Canoeing, carriage rides, fishing on St. Joseph River/lakes.

Rates $75-$105

DEWEY LAKE

Shady Shores Resort   **(616) 424-5251**
      COTTAGES

This resort is located on Dewey Lake, 30 miles east of Benton Harbor. Completely furnished and equipped housekeeping cottages have electric ranges, refrigerators, heat, private bath, blankets and cooking/eating utensils. Also included are boats, bicycles, playground, badminton, shuffleboard, croquet, and tennis. Safe swimming on private sandy beach. $150 deposit.

Weekly $260-$370

HAGAR SHORES

The Sand Castles   **(800) 972-0080**
      COTTAGES

Ten housekeeping cottages sleep from 2 to 10. Each has a kitchenette or full kitchen w/cooking utensils, coffee maker and toaster, ceiling fans, some separate living/dining/kitchen areas w/microwave. Bedding included (bring your own towels). Cable hook-up offering HBO. Lake Michigan beaches, restaurants nearby.

Weekly $200-$500

MICHIGAN COTTAGES • CHALETS • CONDOS • B&B'S

KALAMAZOO

HALL HOUSE
LIZ & BOB COSTELLO

(616) 343-2500
BED & BREAKFAST

Premier lodging in National Historic District. Business/leisure travelers will find this Georgian-style city inn unmatched. A sanctuary in the city where polished mahogany, gleaming marble and roaring fireplaces await. Near College/University, theater, shopping and dining. Private baths and phones, TV. AC. 4 rooms.

Daily $45-$120

LAKESIDE

THE PEBBLE HOUSE
JEAN & ED LAWRENCE

(616) 469-1416
BED & BREAKFAST

1912 Craftsman style buildings connected by wooden walkways and pergolas. Furnished with arts and crafts style antiques. Fireplaces, rocker filled porches, wild flower gardens, tennis court. Lake Michigan beach access. Scandinavian style breakfast. Suites. Outdoor smoking only. 7 rooms with private baths.

Daily $80-$136

LAWRENCE

BLUEWATER COTTAGES

(616) 674-8479
COTTAGES

On 5 scenic acres overlooking Lake Reynolds with 320 ft. of sandy beach. House-keeping cottages offer 1-2 bedrooms w/living rooms, fully equipped kitchens, and bathrooms w/showers. Use of a boat is included. Enjoy swimming, boating, fishing, badminton, horseshoes, and cozy evening campfires by the lake.

Weekly $225-$350

OAK COVE RESORT

(616) 674-8228 • (708) 983-8025
HISTORIC LODGE/COTTAGES/HOMES

Nestled on 16 wooded acres overlooking beautiful Lake Cora. Seven cottages (no kitchens), 7 lodge rooms plus 3 spacious homes (includes full kitchens and living area). All linens provided. Hiking trails, bicycling, flea markets, sandy beach, antiques, fishing, boats, *free* golf. 3 hearty meals like mother used to make included in price.

Weekly $315   Daily $67.50

Editor's Note: Beautiful lake view, friendly owners, great food and plenty to do ... at prices to make your pocketbook smile ... everything you need for a perfect getaway. See our review this issue!

MENDON

MENDON COUNTRY INN   (616) 496-8132
DICK & DOLLY BUERKLE   BED & BREAKFAST

EDITOR'S ★ CHOICE!

Overlooking the St. Joseph River, this romantic country inn has antique filled guest rooms with private baths. Free canoeing, bicycles built for two, fifteen acres of woods and water. Restaurant and Amish Tour guide. Featured in Country Living and Country Home magazines. 7 Jacuzzi suites w/fireplace. 18 rooms.

Daily $65-$150

Editor's Note: Reviewed in 1993-94. The Buerkle's will definitely make you feel at home! Charming historic inn. Their Creekside Lodge rooms with 2-person Jacuzzi, fireplace and plenty of privacy make for one romantic stay!

PLAINWELL

THE 1882 JOHN CRISPE HOUSE   (616) 685-1293
ORMAND & NANCY LEFEVER   BED & BREAKFAST

Museum quality Victorian elegance, on the Kalamazoo River, featuring original gaslight fixtures, plaster medallions, samples of 1882 furnishings. Between Grand Rapids and Kalamazoo off U.S. 131. Close to some of western Michigan's finest gourmet dining, golf, skiing, and antique shops. Full breakfast. A/C. Visa/MC. Gift certificates. 5 rooms. No smoking/alcohol/pets. "A step back in time."

Daily $40-$95

SAUGATUCK

BAYSIDE INN   **(800) 548-0077 • (616) 857-4321**
KATHY & FRANK WILSON   **BED & BREAKFAST**
Once a charming boat house, now a contemporary B&B. Watch the water
activity during the summer or gather around the cozy fireplace in the winter.
Located on the water in downtown Saugatuck with 6 guest rooms and two
efficiency apartments, all with private bath, private decks. 8 rooms.

Daily $55-$165 Double

GOSHORN LAKE RESORT   **(800) 541-4210 • (616) 857-4808**
RIC GILLETTE   **COTTAGES**
Sixteen housekeeping cottages from rustic to deluxe. Some with wood burning
fireplaces, AC. Fully equipped kitchens, picnic tables & BBQ grill. Beautiful
sandy, private swimming beach, volleyball, horseshoes, basketball, fire pit
area, and boat rentals. Near Saugatuck, Lake Michigan beaches and golf.
Nearby hiking trails, x-country skiing.

Weekly $350-$623   Daily $60-$125

THE KIRBY HOUSE   **(616) 857-2904**
LOREN & MARSHA KONTIO   **BED & BREAKFAST**
The most popular bed and breakfast in the Saugatuck/Douglas area. Furnished
with antiques of the 1890's. Most rooms with private baths, air conditioning and
fireplace rooms available. Pool, hot tub and bicycles. Full breakfast buffet. Near
shopping and Lake Michigan. Advanced Reservations imperative.

Daily $65-$100 Dbl.

THE PARK HOUSE   **(800) 321-4535 • (616) 857-4535**
LYNDA & JOE PETTY   **BED & BREAKFAST**
On National Historic Register. Saugatuck's oldest residence (1857) hosted
Susan B. Anthony. Queen beds and private baths. Fireplace, A/C, close to
town, beach and ski trails. Two luxury suites and Rose Garden Cottage offer
jet tubs and fireplaces. More than a night's stay—a homecoming! 9 rooms.

Daily $75-$160

WICKWOOD COUNTRY INN   **(616) 857-1465**
JULEE ROSSO-MILLER & BILL MILLER   **BED & BREAKFAST**
A charming European-style Inn located in the beautiful Victorian Village of
Saugatuck on the Eastern Shores of Lake Michigan. Owner Julee Rosso-Miller,
serves up breakfast and hors d'oeuvres daily using recipes from her four best
selling cookbooks. "The Silver Palate", "The Silver Palate Good Times", "The
New Basics" and "Great Good Foods".

Daily $100-$175

ST. JOSEPH

SAND RABBIT BEACH HOUSE
(616) 468-3835
BEACH HOUSE

This 3 bedroom Lake Michigan beach house is fully furnished and features CATV, A/C, microwave, washer/dryer, enclosed yard and deck. Sleeps up to 6. Includes 1 king WB — loft has large floor pillows and sleeping bags. Only 5 min. from downtown St. Joseph. $200 deposit (per week). No pets. No smoking.

Call for Rates

THE SILVERBEACH FUNHOUSE
(616) 983-2959
CONDOS\

If you enjoy crystal clear waters and broad sandy beaches, this is for you! Your quaint, clean cottage is just a stones throw away from the ever popular silver beach on Lake Michigan. *The Cup* (upstairs) sleeps 4. *The Saucer* (downstairs) sleeps 10. Enjoy swimming, fishing, boogie boarding, wind surfing, shopping, free concerts. Reserve early.

Weekly   **Cup** (upstairs) $550   **Saucer** (downstairs) $800

Editor's Note: Comfortable rooms, fun decor and great location make this a good choice! See our review this issue.

SOUTH CLIFF INN BED & BREAKFAST
BILL SWISHER
(616) 983-4881
BED & BREAKFAST

Overlooking Lake Michigan, this traditional brick home has luxurious accommodations with a relaxed atmosphere. Each room has been tastefully decorated with a combination of traditional and antique furnishings. Relax on the private beach just steps away. Enjoy a continental breakfast in the lakeside sun room.

Room with whirlpool tub, plus, suite with fireplace available. A/C. 7 rooms.

Daily (Seasonal) $75-$115

SHERWOOD

UNION LAKE RESORT, INC.
FRANK & RUTH MORFORD
(517) 741-3146
COTTAGES

Eight units, some rustic log cabins, others fully carpeted and paneled, 2 with double beds, fully equipped kitchen, and bathroom w/shower. Bring your own towels,

UNION LAKE RESORT, INC. (continued...)

bedding, and blankets. Each cottage has a rowboat. On property are groceries and fishing needs. The resort is situated on a high bank with 20 steps to the lake.

Daily $32.50   Weekly $162.50

SOUTH HAVEN

A COUNTRY PLACE COTTAGES AND BED & BREAKFAST   (616) 637-5523
ART & LEE NIFFENEGGER   COTTAGES PLUS BED & BREAKFAST

An 1860's Greek Revival bed and breakfast features five lovely guest rooms, private baths and full breakfast. Also available are three charming cottages featuring fresh pine interiors maintained with care and accented in a relaxing country theme. Cottages offer 1-2 bedrooms, full kitchens and private baths. Cottages open May-Oct. B&B open year around. 2 cottages offer direct beach access—remaining cottage and B&B beach access 1/2 block away. Beach accessed through stairway.

Cottages $450-$700 (weekly)   Bed & Breakfast $50-$85 (daily)

Editor's Note: Gracious owners, sparkling clean accommodations and charming decorations — all of the Niffenegger's lodging are outstanding! See our review in this edition! P.S. We liked their cat, Munchken, too!

ARUNDEL HOUSE—AN ENGLISH B&B   (616) 637-4790
PAT & TOM ZAPAL   BED & BREAKFAST

This turn-of-the-century resort home has been fully restored and is registered with the Michigan Historical Society. Guest rooms decorated with antiques and maintained in English tradition. Continental buffet breakfast and afternoon tea. Walking distance to beach, restaurants, shops, marinas.

Daily $45-$80

Editor's Note: Delightful B&B ! See our review in this edition.

COTTAGE AT GLEN HAVEN SHORES   (616) 455-5602
ANDREA KULDANEK   COTTAGE

Cottage on Lake Michigan Bluff between Saugatuck and South Haven. One bedroom and sleeping loft (accommodates 8), full bath. Fully equipped kitchen, wood burning stove, VCR, screened porch. Access to tennis court. Bike trail nearby. Provide your own linens & paper products. Available May-Oct. No smoking. No pets.

Weekly $800   (Weekend rates available after Labor Day)

LAST RESORT B&B INN

(616) 637-8943
BED & BREAKFAST

Originally built in 1883 as South Haven's first resort inn. Watch Lake Michigan sunsets from the deck. Most rooms offer views of Lake Michigan or the harbor. Penthouse suites provide best views and feature Jacuzzi's. A/C. Open April-Oct. 14 rooms with private baths.

Daily $45-$175

LOKNATH-CHANDERVARMA, HARBOR'S UNIT #32

(616) 344-3012
CONDO

Two bedroom/2 bath condo (sleeps 7). Elegantly furnish, large master bedroom offers queen bed. Features air conditioning, CATV, fully equipped kitchen w/microwave and dishwasher. Panoramic view with private beach, pool, laundry, garage. Provide your own towel and linens. Minimum 7 day stay. Available year around. No pets.

Weekly $850 (May-Sept.)

MICHI-MONA-MAC

(616) 637-3003 • (708) 982-1433
COTTAGES

You'll see truly spectacular sunsets from the pure, spotless beach. Very clean and well maintained cottages features full kitchens, private baths, ceiling fans. Beachside rooms feature lovely bay windows and fireplace.

Weekly $700 (and up)

Editor's Note: The beach here is small but lovely. Plain exterior of cottages deceiving (narrow row of apartment-linked units divided by a cement walkway). Interiors small but very clean, well maintained with all the "fixings"! New bay windows in beachfront units terrific! Sandy incline gets you to water.

NORTH BEACH INN & PIGOZZI'S

(616) 637-6738
INN

1890's Victorian styled B&B overlooks Lake Michigan Beach. All rooms offer private baths. Restaurant, Pigozzi, serves full breakfasts, lunch and dinners.

Call for Rates

PARK PLACE
MERYL GREENE

(616) 637-6400
COTTAGE

Three bedroom (sleeps 6) sits on a quiet side street within 1-1/2 blocks from beach. Short walk to town and marinas. Linens provided (bring towels). Newer bathroom/shower. Includes telephone, fully equipped kitchen, color cable TV. Ceiling fans. If staying consecutive weeks, maid service is provided on Saturday. Outside hot/cold shower available for rinsing sand off from beach, etc. Monthly rentals in fall and winter (rate negotiable).

Weekly $575 (July, August)

MICHIGAN COTTAGES • CHALETS • CONDOS • B&B'S

RIVERBEND RETREAT
(616) 637-3505
COTTAGE

Secluded cedar cottage on beautiful Black River. Stone fireplace, hot tub, boat dock, canoe, boat. Fully equipped for 10-12 people. Dishwasher, phone, TV. Towels and bedding provided. Open year around.

Call for Rates

THE SEYMOUR HOUSE
CAROLYN FRAZIER & LEOPOLDO AMIGO
(616) 227-3918
BED & BREAKFAST

Be pampered by European hospitality in the surroundings of a Victorian mansion. Full breakfast, late afternoon tea, rooms decorated with old world antiques, private baths, A/C, 10 acres with trails for your enjoyment all year round. In ground swimming pool and large stocked pond. 5 rooms. Guest cabin also available.

Daily $68-$138

SLEEPY HOLLOW RESORT
(616) 637-1127
COTTAGES/APARTMENTS/DUPLEX

This 58 years old Art Deco style resort provides the "all in one" family vacation. Theater, restaurant and plenty of activities on the resort premises to keep you busy. Cottages and apartments include partial to full kitchens, private baths.

Weekly $450-$1,040

Editor's Note: Lots of activities at this American Plan resort. See our review in this edition!

TANBITHN
MARCIA ROBINSON
(616) 637-4304
COTTAGE

One bedroom (sleeps 5) cottage on North Shore Drive. Features CATV, telephone, ceiling fan and room air conditioning. Fully renovated in 1994 including bathroom fixtures, kitchen area. Linens provided (bring towels). Light and airy interior with wicker highlights. Only 1/2 block from beach, 1 block from marina. Fall/winter rates negotiable.

Weekends $110 (per night)   Weekly $700 (May -Sept.)

THOMPSON HOUSE
JOYCE THOMPSON
(616) 637-6521
HOME

Charming home, sleeps six. One block to South Beach, Riverfront Park. Great garden, umbrella table, wraparound porch and deck. Enjoy all the modern conveniences including microwave, dishwasher, laundry, central air, electronic air cleaner, a water purifier and whirlpool bathtub.

Weekly $750   Holidays $850

Editor's Note: This is a very well maintained home on a quiet and lovely side street. A great place to be away from the maddening crowds.

Twin Peaks on Park
Meryl Green

(616) 637-6400
Cottages

Side-by side, mirror image, these two cottages sit in close proximity to each other on a quiet side street. Each with 2 bedrooms, ceiling fans, plus sofa beds (sleeps 7). Newer kitchens and bath. Separate dining room. Telephone, cable TV, microwave. Shared washer and dryer. Webber grill. Fully equipped including linens. Only 1-1/2 blocks from beach.

Weekly $575 (July-August)

Victoria Resort B & B
Bob & Jan

(800) 473-7376 • (616) 637-6414
Cottages/Bed & Breakfast

This 3 acre family resort has 17 cottages/rooms available. It is located one block from lake Michigan Beach and was renovated the fall of 1993, and feature 2-3 bedroom cottages plus B&B rooms. Includes A/C, CATV, VCR, full kitchen, linens provided, playground area, and evening bonfires. Full maid service. B&B rooms range from cozy to spacious. Some rooms with whirlpools

Weekly   Cottages from $750   Rooms from $49

Editor's Note: Comfortable and very clean accommodations for family fun! See our review in this edition!

Yelton Manor Bed & Breakfast
Elaine Herbert & Rob Kripaitis

(616) 637-5220
Bed & Breakfast

On the sunset coast of beautiful Lake Michigan. Seventeen guest rooms with private baths. Some have Jacuzzi and fireplace. Extravagant honeymoon and anniversary suites. Evening hors d' oeuvres, fabulous breakfast and day-long goodies. A true make-yourself-at-home, luxurious getaway.

Daily $90-$195

Editor's Note: A premiere resort for executive retreats. A great way to FORGET ABOUT THE...STRESS! See our review in this edition.

STEVENSVILLE

Chalet on the Lake

(616) 465-6365
Chalets/Condos

51 spacious, well equipped, 2-story duplex chalet-styled lodgings 7 miles south of St. Joseph. Resort offers 27 acres with each A-frame overlooking the water. All lodgings include 2 nicely decorated 2 bedroom condominiums (sleep 8) with full kitchens, dining areas, living rooms (most w/TVs) and patios. Resort features nature trails, volleyball, 5 tennis courts, 2 pools and large beach. Bring towels. Open year around.

Weekly $500-$800

UNION CITY

VICTORIAN VILLA INN (800) 34-VILLA • (517) 741-7383
RONALD J. GIBSON **BED & BREAKFAST**

This romantic, 19th Century Intalianate style B&B is a perfect spot for anniversaries or any other special occasion. Their tower suites, with private parlor, offers an excellent birds-eye view of the town. Their restaurant features menus which reflect the tastes and trends of the 19th century and are sure to please. Private baths. 10 rooms.

Daily $75-$125

UNION PIER

GARDEN GROVE B&B (616) 469-6346
BED & BREAKFAST

Built in 1925 this B&B has a rambling summer cottage feel. The surrounding country gardens have been brought indoors with uniquely decorated rooms in garden themes. Outdoor decks and balconies. Two whirlpool suites. Outdoor hot tub. Fireplaces, bicycles, tasty breakfasts. 4 rooms with private baths.

Daily $70-$130

PINE GARTH INN (616) 469-1642
RUSS & PAULA BULIN **BED & BREAKFAST/COTTAGES**

EDITOR'S ★ CHOICE!

Restored summer estate and cottages, located in a quiet setting overlooking Lake Michigan. All guest rooms have spectacular lake views. Rooms have queen beds, private baths, VCR. Cottages have 2 bedrooms, kitchens, fireplace, hot tubs, gas grills and private decks with beach chairs. 7 rooms, 5 cottages.

	Rooms*	Cottages*
Daily	$105-$140	$195-$225

* In season. Call for off-season rates.

Editor's Note: Great views and wonderful guest rooms.

THE INN AT UNION PIER (616) 469-4700
JOYCE ERICKSON PITTS & MARK PITTS **BED & BREAKFAST**

An elegant Inn blending barefoot informality with the comforts of a well-appointed country home. Lake Michigan is across the street. Most rooms have porches and Swedish fireplaces. Relax in our sauna or outdoor hot tub. Linger over homemade breakfast. Hosting corporate retreats. Private baths. 16 rooms. Weekday specials. No smoking. No pets.

Daily $105-$175

INDEX
BY CITY/LAKE/AREA

MICHIGAN COTTAGES • CHALETS • CONDOS • B&B'S

Send Us Your Comments!

We're always looking to improve this publication. So, let us know if our book was helpful — what improvements you'd like to see in our next edition — and your opinion of the place(s) you've stayed. *We look forward to hearing from you!*

Do you have property you'd like to list in our next publication?

If you have a property in Michigan that you would be interested in listing, please send your name, address, phone number, along with a brief description of your property. We'll have you complete one of our Property Owner's Questionnaires and add you to our contact list. We'll be sure to notify you when we update the next edition!

Need Additional Copies of the Michigan Vacation Guide????

If you'd like to order additional copies of our Guide, please send $10.95 *plus* $2.50 tax and shipping to TR Desktop Publishing c/o The Michigan Vacation Guide at the below address:

THE MICHIGAN VACATION GUIDE

TR Desktop Publishing
P.O. Box 180271
Utica, Michigan 48318-0271
(810) 228-8780